A281

£1.50

D1395062

THE DIARY
OF A
FARMER'S WIFE
1796–1797

ANNE HUGHES

ALLEN LANE

Allen Lane
Penguin Books Ltd
536 King's Road
London SW10 OUH

First published in the *Farmers Weekly* 1937
Published by Countrywise Books 1964
Published by Allen Lane 1980
Reprinted 1980
Copyright © Mollie Preston, 1937, 1964, 1980

The publishers regret that it is impossible to give
acknowledgement to the illustrator, whom they have
been unable to trace.

ISBN 0 7139 1327 4

Set in Monotype Caslon
Printed in Great Britain by
Billing & Sons Ltd.,
London, Guildford and Worcester

꧁ ꧂

'Anne Hughes, her boke in wiche I write what
I doe, when I hav thee tyme, and beginnen wyth this
daye, Feb ye 6 1796.'

꧁

CONTENTS

To begin the story of how Anne Hughes' diary came into existence, we must go back to 1896, to the time when a young girl of twelve called Jeanne Keyte was living on a Herefordshire farm. Jeanne, who is ultimately responsible for the present existence of the diary, was born in 1884 to Mary and Edward Keyte, tenant farmers at a Gloucestershire farm, probably called Upper Coscombe, Didbrook, Whinchcombe. Jeanne was sent at an early age to live with a young cousin on a farm which was possibly Manor Farm, Ballingham, near Ross-on-Wye. (Several details are not absolutely certain.) She probably went as a companion to her lonely cousin who was an only child.

While she was there, Jeanne met Mary Anne Thomas who had previously been Mary Anne Hughes, a very bright lady in her eighties. Jeanne at this time was ten or twelve. Mary Anne would read to the girl from a thin book containing very fine spidery writing: this was her mother, Anne Hughes', 'Boke'. Mary Anne also related many of her mother's stories which Jeanne then wrote down because she always thought, 'Some day I'll want to put them in a book.'

Jeanne was educated to grammar school level and left Herefordshire when she married in 1907/8, probably against the wishes of the Herefordshire family, who thought her husband was not good enough. Her husband was a farm manager, and like Jeanne he came from a long line of farmers.

As Jeanne Preston she wrote occasional articles in the 1930s for the *Farmers Weekly*. The editor requested something that could be run as a serial, so Jeanne thought of Anne Hughes and assembled her various sources which included

Anne Hughes' Boke and the notes she had taken herself when a girl. It could well be that she decided to present it in the form of a diary rather than as a series of disconnected incidents, or it is possible that the original was actually in diary form into which Jeanne then arranged all her stories.

One source for some, but not all, of the recipes was a thick old book that had belonged to Jeanne's mother, Mary Keyte. None of the original work can now be found. The old cookery book was admired by a cousin and Jeanne, being of an impulsive and generous nature, immediately gave it to him and it is now lost.

Anne Hughes' Boke may well be in America. One story suggests that it was given to an American airman during the Second World War.

The necklace, always referred to as Anne Hughes' necklace by Jeanne, was sold for the war effort and fetched £170.

Many people have tried to trace various characters from the Diary but invariably without success. This is not really surprising when you consider that a young girl was taking notes from an old lady and such things as the spelling of names may have been inaccurately recorded.

How should Anne Hughes' Boke be regarded? Certainly it should not stand as a historical text in the conventional sense. Personally, I think of it like a folk song, something that has existed for many years in the countryside. A folk song carries the true voice of the past; it has passed through many voices and ears and each person has contributed something. Anne Hughes' Boke has passed through two later people but the original person is still there, shining through. It is the authentic voice of the farmer's wife, a record to stand for the lives of many women on remote farms, a way of life that has finally changed.

MICHAEL CROUCHER – 1979

ANNE HUGHES AND MISTRESS ELLIS

❧

Today hav John and I bin wed this 3 yere and here I do set down all that I do every day.

Today I did do my butter maken, leving Sarah to cook most of the dinner, as the butter was longe time cummin, indeed not till John had put in a crown piece and turned did it cum. Sarah did burne the dinner, like she always do, and John was very cross therebye, he mislyking Sarahs cooken, so I do sometimes hav to let him think it is me. Men be verry tiresome sometimes.

Feb. ye 8. – This morn John in with the newes that Parson Willum Ellis will preche at our church cum Sunday, and will ette with us, for which I be sorrie for he do ette so much mete, it do give me much work cooken. John likes to hav a good table when folkes do cum, so carters wiffe and Sarah will have to help me. I shall wear my purple silk cum Sunday. John bein the biggest farm-holder here-about I do hav to keep up with it, but it does wearie my whiles.

A 'BUSSYE' DAY FOR THE HUGHES HOUSEHOLD

Feb. ye 9. – Today hav been a bussye one. Sarah, carters wiffe and me have cooked most of to-morrowes dinner and supper toe, which Parson Ellis be sure to stopp, etting and drinking all the time. But I do think there be enuff for I have boiled a sadell of mutten, 3 capons, and a round of spised beefe and a roste hare with his inside filled with herbes and bitts; then some tartes and a pritch pudden, some cheese and butter and bredd. Thys with pertaties and greens and other

trymmings should do verrie well. And there will be cyder and
beere and sherrie wine to drink. After I will sett in the parlur
like a ladie and lett Sarah put on the tay, while I shall worrit
in case she does brake the dyshes.

LADY SUSAN'S WAY OF COOKING A LEG OF MUTTON

Parson Ellis and John doe talk verrie dry, but I do hav to sett
with them, John thinking it be the propper thing for me to
doe. But later I shall say I must see that tee be getting reddy
and I must cut the cake; which is already done by Sarah, but
John not noeing this I can get away. I do hope Mistress
Ellis will not cum, she bein so fussie; but if she do, I shall hav
a dish wich will make her want to noe about, I be bound. For
I hav cooked my mutton this way like the Lady Susan did
tell me she doe have ett cooked in her own kitchen.

I do from the leg cut out a thick slice verrie carefull, then
I do fill it with a mess made of a cutte up union, tyme, and
parsley, and 2 egges cooked hard. This be all chopt up together with some fatte bacon. Then I do push all into the
mutton and press in the cutt-out piece, and tie it hard with
twine to hold it furm, wile it doe cook. When it be cold I doe
take away the twine and it do cut out furm.

SO MISTRESS ELLIS HAD TO WALK TO CHURCH, TOO

If Mistress Ellis do cum, I shall give her some but shall not
tell her what makes the fyne flavour, she bein sure to quiss;
but I shall not say, so she will be madd.

I have no more time to rite now, but go to bedd.

Feb. ye 10. – Parson and Mistress Ellis come earlie and did ett

12

a good meal of bread and cheese, and did drink 2 juggs of cyder. Then we to church after me tellen Sarah what to doe, and where to putt the dishes on the tabel. Mistress Ellis comin I did fetch out all my silver and glass so to make a shine, she haven littel to her name as I do know. There was much mudd to walk in to church. John not haven a cart out on the Sabbeth day, we futts it. She minsed along aside me prating of her new cloathes and that the gown she is waring cost so much, which I doe know is onlie her last yeres turned about and new bowes on for show. This I cappes by saying I will show her my new brockade which John brought me last market day, he havin got the better of old Skinnie-flinte Tom over some hay he did sell him. She be verrie jellous, not ansuring when I do tell her of the new gown. The sermon very dry, with some hard nockes at the folks which he do not like. John did nod and I did praye that Sarah would not brake the dishes, or ett any of the little things which she doe some wiles, when my back be turned. Sermon lasted 2 houres, then we out and home to dinner. I did see Farmer Wells and his mistress looking prosperous, he no doubt have sold his straw, so a few ginneas to spend. Verrie glad was I to see Sarah had done all verrie well, the tabel lookinge good; and I did see Mistress Ellis was imprested by my glass and silver forkes and spoones, albeit she nott wanting to show it but woode have us think hers was as good, which I do doubt.

SO I SHOWED HER MY SYLK, WITH WHITE SPOTTES

A greate lot eeten, she having 3 bigg slivers off the mutten, and pestering me the wye and warefore off the new taste, which I do turn off by saying the wether be well for the time of the yer; until I could see she was wroth trying not to show it outards, saying that she would ett no more; bein afraid the flavor would disagree with her, which I doute not, she ettin so much.

After we had dined, I did take her to my sleepin chamber to showe off on her my best cloes; at seein which, she begins to trump up about her new black sylk which had cost so much, and which I do know she did buy off Mary Ann herself telling me so. Knowing this I could well afford to bring out my black sylk with the white spottes, what John did buy for me and which I had not put on. This did end her bounce so down again, it being two howers since she had fed, to tee drinken.

PARSON WILLUM ELLIS GOES HOME
'A LITTLE PEART'

She did offer to help, butt I tell her Sarah do know what to do, me knowing well that Madam did only want to see my larder shelfs, she bein a nosie person.

So into the parlur, where Sarah busie; mee hitchen to help, but did not, bein a ladye for the day.

After tee drinking, did start to hint it would soon be dark. And she did fish for a night visit, which I made not to hear; and did pack her up a bag of eggs and butter as a hint to be gone. Which they both did, to our content; we bein tired to their caddel. He a little peart with Johns wine did go home tittering; but she verrie prim and proper. We in to the kitchen where I did ketch Sarah ettin a slice of ham; which I forgave her as she had praised me in front of Mistress Ellis, which pleased me. John cummin in to see what vittles was left, he did lock it up. So we to bed, me bein tired.

MARKET FOR JOHN — HOUSEWORK FOR ANNE

Feb. ye 12. — To-day bein market day, John goes to sell 2 fat cowes. So Sarah and me do sett about and clere out the cupboards, finding much dust therein. We did also scrub the passages and kitchens, then clere up the parlur and furniture, which do look all the better.

We did then sett us downe to dinner, ett bein mid-day. We did hav a rabbit pye cold and some pig-mete, with cheese and bread. Sarah bein hungrie did ett a good dinner; pyking the mete off the bones with her teeth, for which I reproved her – but la, in 2 minnets she at it again. But then the pye was good for I did make it verrie well.

After dinner we to the dairy to scower shelves and pannes and such like; then the floor.

Then Sarah out to milk the cow Betsy, which do always kick John over, soe Sarah does it; I to feed the calves and to watch Bill Jones feed the pigges, which he do slip if we not there to see him. John feares he do help his own pigg with the meal, but I think he hath not the wit, being a dimmel body and slow.

TESTIMONIAL FROM A PLEASED HUSBAND

Then I to the kitchen to see all is reddy for John's home cummin, the while Sarah do feed the hens; which do set up a fine ado when they do see us. She comes in later with a fine goose egg, the first this yere; which I do put in the pan and cook for John's tee, with 2 good slivvers of ham; and do put the boiled beef and cheese withe a meat pastie, he bein always verrie empty when he do cum from market. It bein a cold day I do get reddy a good bowl of punch steaming hot, which is as well, for he cummen in verrie cross with the newes of not sellen one of the cowes which he do bring back.

Later being fed he tells me his mother will be cummin in 2 dayes time to visit us. This do please me, she bein verrie kind and good to me always. Me saying this to John, he is verrie pleased, and do say how he did like the goose egg, and what a good wife he hav got, to which I do agree, seeing how I do put up with his fandilles and temper without saying a word. But this I shall not tell him.

Later I and Sarah to our sewing, and John to look at the yards to see all is safe; then a good supper and to bed.

SARAH DISCOVERS HER VALENTINE

Feb. ye 14. – This be Saint Val's day and this morn I did see Sarah cum in from the milking looking all red about the cheek and her cap awry. I bein curious did stop her, and she did say Carter Trues son did say he was her Valentine, and she had said yes. She did giggel a great deal and I did tell her to get on with her work, and not to be a silly wench; but I fear me there will be much whisperings and kissen going on, they bein both young.

I must be watchful of Sarah and see she do not neglect the calfs and pigges and hens, which do now lay good egges; which is good for me, as John do let me keep hen monies for my pokett, which do suit me much.

಼ 2 ಼

ANNE MAKES THE BACON

಼

Feb. ye 16. – Johns mother didd come today, riding pack-horse so to keep an eye on the wagon, to which she did carry divers thinges. A spinette for me, to me joy, me bein abel to play upon it, havin learned off Mistress Prue. It do look verrie fine in my parlour, nearby the greate chair Johns father did give us when we were wed. A new bonnet she did bring; and soe am I greatly pleased therebye.

She did first drink a good hot glass of punch, it bein verrie cold, and she on the road all yesterday; breakin her journey at cousen Emma for the night's rest. She also did send me a packet of eggs, which did please me mightily; bein abel to sell them, and so add to my stocken – I saying naught to John, he bein none the wiser.

JOHN'S MOTHER WILL HELP

John do think now his mother be here it be time to kill the pigges for our this year's bacon, she bein most useful to help with all to do with pigge. So I do be thinking how to place the joints: some for the salten led, and some for to ette sweet and green. Mistress Prue and her sister Mistress Livvy must hav a little joint, as they allus does, but I shall keep the chittlings. We do all like them, and Sarah will ette up any oddses there be left. John do allus get a sickey turn when we do kill pigges; he do like the new meat so much, so do ette to his filling. I do tell him he should nowe better.

We did not go to church this day, bein bussie with Johns mother; so to bed early.

IN THE SALTEN LEDS

Feb. ye 18. – Up betimes this morn, to put the pots on, filled with water, to boil hot for toe clean the pigges when they be killed.

Carters wife do come to help, and to clean the pigges innerds; a messie job that I do mislike. But they be verrie good when cooked. We do boil them in the big pot 3 dayes after they be well soaked in brine water.

The pigges be hung up in the pot-kitchen to cool till tomorrow, when they will be cut up and the meat cut from out them inside. The flytches be then put in the salten leds and

17

rubbed with a mess made with 3 punds of salt, 3 punds of black sugar and some saltpetter and soda. This bee well rubbed on the fleshy sides, which is left till cum 3 dayes; then we do turn them over, putting more salt, and turn about for 3 weekes: we do drain off the brine, and hange in the chimblie corner to dry.

4 SHILLEN A WEEK

We did have a bussie time, and John did cut his thumbe, and silly old Joe Tombes did slip and sit in the pan of boiling water, and did youpe about because it did go hot to his britches. We did have fried liver and fat from the pigge for our supper. I fear me much that John will ette to his discomfort, as he do sometimes, he bein a big man and hartie. I did write all this whiles he do sleep in bed, so now I to bed too, verrie tired.

Feb. ye 19. – To the lard makin early. Johns mother did cut up all the fat whilst Sarah did take away all the skinny bits. Then the fat was put in the big pan and melted, Sarah sturring it so not to burn.

I did give old Joe some odd bits, warning him not to tell John, which he says faithfully not to. John dislikes given to the farm folks, saying it do spoil them, they being paid 4 good shillen a week, and let to keep a pigge.

WE PREPARE FOR A PARTY

All the meat do make a goodly show set out on the pantrie slabs. Today did Parson Ellises madam send her grettins to me, and her rubbishy love, by Emma Jones; who do come to the washen this week, we bein bussie. Madam hav likely heard of the pigge killin and do hope for a passel of meat, which she will not get. I sendin her the pigges feet to be rid of them; I knowing right well she do hate them, havin no teeth to bite them, bein so froustic.

I did pack up a nice joint and send to my ladie Susan at the Big House today, she bein back from London town now. And John do say we be to havin naybours to sup with us, to help ett up the bits. So mother and me hav made a goodlie lot of pyes and such ready. Later to bed, bein sick of the pigges; Johns mother and Sarah likewise. John verrie grumpy, so I fear he hav etten too much pigge.

Feb. ye 21. – Today I did hav to giv John a dose of fissicke for his good, as I had feared I should. I did giv him the jouce of a lemmon with a pinch of ginger, and blacke pepper, and a taste of salt; which I did make him drink after swallowing some pepper corns. He did make a mighty fuss, sayen I should kill him with my messes, burnin his innards. But it always do him good.

Johns mother and me and Sarah hav set the best parlour to rights ready for the party this next day. Farmer Bliss and his wiffe be cummin, and Mistress Prue and her sister Livvy. We do like them much, they bein real ladies, their father bein the squire when he did die. Parson Jones and Johns friend Tom and his cozen Artie, so we shall bee a party. I be glad Parson Jones be back, so we shall not hav Ellis and his frustie madam to the church anon.

We hav set a goodly store for them: there be pyes and tartes and pastries, roast pigge meat and a great ham and apple pudden; with a goose with a goodly stuffin in his insyde to giv a flayvour and chese fresh from the vatte.

John hav put a tap to the new barrel of beer, and there will be cyder and sherrie wine, and I shall bring out a bottel of my cowslip wine as well as one of Eldernberrie for the ladies. So we should do verrie well.

John and the menfolk will hav a jar of terbacca, which I do hate the smell of, but do keep them in good fettel.

MADAM ELLIS'S SCANDAL

I do not ask Parson Ellis and his madam, I hearing that she did giv the pigges trotties to a baudley woman in the street, telling that they be too tuff to ett theirselfes, thee pigges bein old grandames – she knowing well that I should hear tell. To which newes I do say that it do show the company she do keep, knowing full well she will hear it; to my content, for I mislike her much; she do for ever rile me with her primms and prissums – albeit a nobody, her family bein only poor millers tho she do set up to be a lady. John be rid of his bad stomick, and we to bed early, ready for next day.

ॐ 3 ॐ

ANNE ENTERTAINS

ॐ

Feb. ye 25. – I bein wearie did not write in my book till now. The party did go off verrie well. I did play a merrie jigge on the spinette, which did please all vastly; John bein verrie proud at my skill, he knowing well that I did larn off Mistress Prue, as well as to write and reckon monies.

She did play some pretty bits, so we all verrie merrie.

After we had all etten our fill, we to dancing; and Farmer Bliss did sing, as did divers others. Then Parson Jones did tell us a ghost tale that did make my hair to rise; but Mistress Livvy did laff and say it was batter, and we did pass the wine and all did get verrie merrie before they did go, in the early howers.

John did bring in a big bowl of hot rum punch; and all did join hands and say good luck, then did touch glasses and drink our healths. Then all did go home, verrie full and well content. Then I to the kitchen, where I did find Sarah fast asleep, she bein tired. I do tell her to lie abed till six of the clock, which did please her. Then we to bed, as soon as John had looked to see what vittles were left, which I fear me was verrie little.

LADY SUSAN BRINGS GIFTS

Feb. ye 28. – To-day the Lady Susan did call to thank us for the joint of pigge meat we did send her, which she did like much, as I thought she would. She did bring me a verrie fine cloak, with lace upon it, which did please me verrie much.

She did also give me a good passel of chany tee, like she do herself drink; and I did thank her right hartilie, it costen too much for me to drink it much.

She did tell me the ladies in London town do dye their hair, but I did see her own was the same as ever, she not bein one to follow the fashion on London town; but do look right well any way, bein a verrie sweet lady and not a bit uppish. She did like my spinette muchly and sayes it be verrie well orni-mented; and did please us greatly by playin upon it with her own hands to our delight.

INCIDENT OF A FIDDLE-STRING

She did tell me of a cooken grate that do have a oven to bake at its side which do oppen with a lid where the cakes and meat can be cooked, but I dout me if it be of any use. I do not think it would do so well as my big oven, where I do make my bread, so shall not worrit John to get me one.

She did go with Johns mother and me to look at the pigges,

and did say how well the hens did look. Then we back to the parlour where we did drink a dish of the chany tee; then she home. Sarah did go carrying a baskit of my eggs, topped with a pot of my preserved fares, which be verrie good. Sarah walks behind as becomes a decent servent wench.

March ye 1. – Today the wind did blow down the big beech tree, and it did almost hit the hen house, so we now sure of a log to our fires.

Sarah did brake a platter, for which I did scold her; at which she did howel and snuffel so much I did at last give her a piece of my plum cake, which did soon content her. John do say there be no more lambs to cum, for which he is glad; for now the sheepeard will go to his own house for warmth and so save our fire.

March ye 3. – It bein Sunday John and me to church in the morn. The sermon verrie good and the singing right heartie. Jim Beck did brake a fiddel string, which did give a loud pop, and did make him look verrie red in the face when her ladie-ship did look up at him and smile.

John did nod asleep and I did poke him in the ribs, for which he were verrie wrath; but bein in God's house, I was safe. Did see my lady Susan when out of church, who did ask me and Johns mother to a tee drinking cum tuesdaye; which pleased us mitily, we bein much favoured. She did speak verrie prettie to Johns mother.

March ye 4. – Up betimes and to the washen, for which the carters wife here at 4 of the clock. After brakefust me to the butter-maken, which did take sum time, it bein verrie cold. Did finish after dinner time.

Johns mother did make a pudden which was verrie good, and John did ett 3 lots, as well as some pigges head. The pudden is made this awayes. You do take some sweet pigge meat and cut it up, then peel and cut up 4 big apples and a carrat into little bits, some sage and a union chopt small, with salt and pepper. Then you do make a paste of flower and butter rubbed together, and mixed with milk. You do roll this out in one piece, then set the mixed mess in the middle and join the ends, making them stick together with milk. Tie up in a cloth, and boil for 3 howers.

Her did make some gravy by boiling bones and herbs verrie well. Carters wiffe and Sarah did hav a platter each for their dinner, which they liked vastly.

Sarah did tell Johns mother that she did like being my maid, she havin good vittles to ett and plentie cloes to her bed. This pleasing me I did give her my blew petticote, not wanton it to wear. Bein tired, we to bed early, and after asleep I to write all this.

WE RETURN A VISIT

March ye 6. – Yesterday we to the Lady Susan to drink tee. We did hav a verrie pleasant time, and did sit in my ladies little parlour; me and Johns mother feeling verrie welcome there. The room was verrie fine, with grand chaires and littel tables. I did see some dust in the chair legs.

She did play some verrie pretty musick on her own spinette, which is bigger than mine, and a very sweet thing. Then we with her up to her bed-chamber to see her new furniture therein. Then to the tee drinking in her parlour, where her futman did wait up on us, as if we were the quality.

I did take my lady a pot of my pickled strawberries, which did please her grately; she not hearing talk of such, and did say would I tell her how to do it. Which I shall write out and send her.

The Lady Susan did walk a piece with us when we home,

which pleased me much, we meeting divers people who did stare to see me in such fine company.

When home we find Sarah with some hot punch ready, it bein verrie cold; for which I did praise her kind thought. And Johns mother did give her a penny piece.

A STRAWBERRY PICKLE

March ye 8. – Have bin bussie this day cleaning out the kitchens and cupboards. Johns mother did shine up the warmen pans and candel sticks maken all look mighty fine when done. After dinner did send Sarah to the big house with the receipt for my lady how to pickle the strawberries.

You do take off the berries verrie sound and ripe, 4 pints; and of sugar 2 pounds, a pint of vinnegar, a stick of cinnamon, and 12 cloves. Boil the spices tied in muslin. After it be stopt boiling on the side of the fire, drop the strawberries in one by one; and put away till next day. Then you do bring all to boiling again and boile for 30 minutes of the clock. Skim off when it do come on the top. Then take out the berries careful from the hot sirup, and the spices too. Then boil the sirup verrie fast until it do go thick, then put back the berries, bring to the boile, then put in hot pots verrie quick and fassen down at once. Sarah did put on a clean apron and her best cloak to do me credit.

She gone, me to her bed-chamber to see if all be clean; which I do find verrie tidy and neat, she bein a good wench; and her bed all ready for the night, and her bed rail put ready for when she do go to bed. She soon back, verrie pleased, saying that my lady herself did speak to her verrie kind; and did thank her for her trouble, and did tell the cook to see she did hav a cup of beer and sum vittels before cuming home agen.

She did also send her regards, and to say she did hope to see me and Johns mother when she do return from taking the waters at Bath. John coming in did here this, he saying my lady is a fine one who be worthy of our respecks, with which I do heartily agree.

March ye 11. – Tomorrow bein Lords day Sarah and me to making pies for dinner, and to cleaning up the kitchens and passages.

In comes Mistress Prue at midday to tell me Joe Shorts wiffe do have a child and she with littel clothes for it, bein verrie poor.

Mistress Prue do say I can help her; which I will most willen, bein sorry for any who do suffer from want. So I with her late to see the poor wretch, and did find her lying most worrie and comfurtless.

I back home to get some clean sheets and a blankit to make the poor sowl better, and some milk for her to drink; which did warm her. We then home with her blessing us.

I did not tell John of me giving her the sheets and blankit, he bein a mere man, so it not wise to do so. Yet I could but think how much better off I be to hav a good bed to lie upon, and plenty of vittels to my inside. I should not like to live in a hovel like Emma Short.

March ye 12. – John to church by himself while I to Emma Shorts cot to wash her. I did cumbe her hair, which was verrie lumpy, did also wipe the babes face and make it tidy and comfurtable, no boddy else doin it.

STRANGE NEWS INDEED

March ye 16. – John did today bring home the cow he did buy off Master Willis. It be a verrie fair beast and do milke easy, my doin it, to please John. He did give 4 ginnes for it which he do fear is a heavy price. But I do think it a fair price for her.

*

March ye 20. – Today John did set the men to thresh the wheat out of the far stack, it being cold and wet they did do it in the barn.

Carters wiffe did come to help with the baking and did bring the news of Gunns cot, in the lane, bein strange of late. She do say that lights have been seen in it, and of groans to be heard after dark, so that some do fear it much. This be strange, the cot bein empty for many months.

She did warn Sarah not to go courting carters lad that road, which did make Sarah giggel much, the silly wench. And I did tell them both to get to their work verrie sharp.

ON A BROOM STICK

April ye 3. – John in with the news of a sick pigge, which I do go out to see. John fears it will die, it bein in a fever and a pinky colour. Then back to the house to find Carters wiffe bussie with the dinner.

I to help her after giving her a mug of cyder and a lump of bread and cheese. After dinner John to sleep, whiles me and Carters wiffe do wash the dishes. She did tell me that Jim the peddler did say he did see a black woman fly out of Gunns cot on a broom stick, with a great black cat sitten on it; where upon he did shake much, and will not go thereto agen. At which I did laugh and say he had drunk over much cyder; but Carters wiffe did think the tale trew.

Me to see Sarah's mother who do seem verrie poorly. She be a nice woman, and do deserve help, for she do work harde to keep her childer. Sarah did offer to come back to feed the piggs and such like, but I did tell her no, to stop home until her sister do come.

ANNE — DISTRICT NURSE

❦

April ye 6. — John to market earlie and me bussie wyth the brede making and so on. Later leaving Carter's wiffe bussie I to Sarah's to see how her mother be, finding her no better, I did send the boy for the doctur to cum, and did give her sum warm milk with a egg beat up in it, the house be verrie clean and tidie did set me down to wait the docturs cuming, who did look verrie grave saying she be in a high fever, and needed blood letting, which me helping him, he did. I did feel verrie sick but did not show it and he did praise me much for being useful. Cums to the door later Mistress Prue who had herd of the sickness, saying she will stop with Sarah till her sister do cum, so I home, to find Carter's wiffe bussie with the milking; and saying she had fed the pigges and hens, I to get the eggs, then indoors to see the tee reddie and the water boiling reddie for the pot. Carter's wiffe works verrie well and can be trusted to do her work well.

Later cums Mistress Prue to say Sarah's sister be cum, and that she feres the mother be no better, and that she herself will stay the night with them. Whereupon I back with her to see what can be done and taking a noggit of brandie in case they do need it. Did find Sarah verrie worried, she telling me she did hear a bell toll over her mother's bed, which she do think means her mother will die; to which I tell her not to think so, but I fear me it may be a warning; then home agen promising to go agen earlie next day, and bidding Sarah to stay home; I managing verrie well with Carter's wiffe, but I do miss Sarah, she being a good maid.

April ye 7. — John cumming in do tell me the pigge be dead and he fears another will die to, which troubles him verrie much. Later cums Sarah's brother to say her mother be much worse, so I do tell Carter's wiffe what to do, and do go back with him, and do find the poor thing verrie much worse and I liked not her looks, not being able to talk to me.

I finding Mistress Prue have been up all night, do tell her to go home and reste and I stay; which she did after me saying I will send the boy if his mother worse; Sarah verrie sad and finding she had been up all night and her sister, did make them both lie down to rest. I staying the while, until Mistress Prue cums in, and I home after her saying she will send to me if poor soul, worse. Later cums Sarah's brother to say will I go agen so I do, to find the pore soul at the last. Mistress Prue and me do wash her pore body and lay her tidie, then me home, taking the 2 little ones to Carter's wiffe to keep a day or two. Death be a sad thing when little childer be left lonlie. I pray God I may be spared to see my own grow up when they do cum.

April ye 12. – I have not writ in my book sum days now, bein bussie helping Sarah and her sister. We did burrie her mother yesterday. It was verrie cold and did rain most all the time. I fear the childer will miss her much, she bein a good mother to them. It bein John's cottage he will let them stop with-out any rent, so the sister will look to them, and he will find work for the lad paying him 2 pense a day, which be a good wage for a lad of 10.

A PIE-MAKING DAY

April ye 14. – John be verrie bussie now and the weather bein fine, the grass be growing well. We did cut the lambs tails yesterday, so today did make pies in my dear mother's way. First we do clean off all the wool, then cut them in littel bittes and stew them verrie slow for 20 minnets by the clock, then I do lay some in a deep platter and season with pepper and salt, then a good layer on the top of sliced apples, some chopt parslie, then more tails and apple and parslie till the platter be fulle, then I do put in some off the broth and cover all wyth a good paste, and do cook it in the oven 1 hower and 20 minnets by the clock; this be verrie nice hot or cold. Carter's wiffe did have sum of the tails as did the shepperd and divers others, and I did send Sarah with a pye all reddie to eat to Mistress Prue, who do like them verrie much.

April ye 16. – John to market today to sell some of the old culls, he not wanting any of the old cowes left, they did make 2 shillings apiece which was not much. My chickens do grow apace now, and my Ladie Susan did send her futman to ask when shall I hav sum for her, she have divers lots everie yere for her tabel, I hav not much time for riting in my book now, being bussie these days.

April ye 18. – Carter's wiffe cummen to do the washen, do tell no boddie will go down the lane at Gunns cott fearing they no not what. John cummen in do say it be nowt at all, only what folks do think, and he will go himself sum day and see; but not he, bee onlie braive words.

CURING JOHN'S 'ILL HUMOUR'

After all work done, me and Sarah to the wood to pick primmy roses for the wine maken; off which there be grate store, we getting 2 bags full, then home again to find John verrie cross at the loss of another sow, so we verrie careful not to cross him. I do get out a bottel of Eldern-berrie wine and warm it up with a beeten egg and cinnamun, of which he be verrie fond, and do soon cure ill-humour. Then Sarah and me do get the primmy roses reddie for the wine, which I do always make same as my dere mother did. This is the waye: of the primmy roses you do take 6 measures from the stalks and crush them in a wooden vat, then slice up 6 lemons and lay on top, then sprinkel 2 handsful of ginger in little bits then another lot of primmy roses, lemmon and ginger bits, put as well 6 sticks of cinnamun, shed over all 2 punds of white sugar, and add 6 pint measures of cold boiled water. Leave til next day, then stir it all up well and add more cold boiled water to cuvver over all, fasten over a cloth and leave it 3 days; then stir everie day for a week, taken care it be the same hower each day, then add 1 quart measure of brandie, stirring all the time. Next day you do put in 6 punds of white sugar and stir till all be melted, then cover and do not touch for another week, after which skim off the top skin and strain all twyce through muslin and put in another quart measure of brandie; put in a verrie clean dry cask and let stand until no more froth do rise; then put in 2 clean egg shells and bung down tightlie for a yere, then put in bottles readdie to drink. It will be a fine drink to use at a partie.

April ye 20. – Cums Master Ellis this morn to ask can he borrow a horse for one day. John saying yes, he do then say will we go and spend a hower cum tomorrow night which we promise. Later did send Sarah with sum oddses from the pantrie for her sister to use, and to see how she does; summen back she do say the peddeler be in the village street, and soon we do here his nock at the door. He do show us his wares, but la, it be but trumprie stuff and no good to me, but I did buy Sarah a broche to wear on her best cloke, and she mity plesed therewith. Then off he did go with a lump of brede and cheese.

The grass be growing fine now in the meadows, and John

31

do think we can soon cut sum albeit a bit erlie, so soon shall we be verrie bussie.

April ye 22. – We to Farmer Ellis yester eve, and a rite good time did we have. Mistress Ellis had layed in a good feed for us to fall to, and we did have a rite merrie time. She haven got the fiddlers in for us to dance, we did tread a measure, and did talk of divers things.

Joe Pringal did say we must see what be rong at Gunns Cott; he not bein afeared, would go himself but for his reumatiz which did stop his runnen; at which we did all laffe, knowing rite well he will not go near in day-lite for fear.

It being late John and me home and he bein perte with drinken the gooseberrie wine did nock agen all the stones with his futte, but he soon abed and asleep, the wile I do rite all this down, then me abed also.

❦ 5 ❦

THE SECRET OF GUNN'S COT

❦

April ye 29. – Yesterday did we have a venturouse time. Telling John and Sarah that after mid-day I going to Mistress Prue, and John saying noute agen it, I off, albeit a bit skeert, to her; taking Johns mubblie stycke to proteck my selfe. After a drinke of wine, we off down the lane to the cott, I feeling verrie muddelie in my stummick, but seeing the other two as usual, I did walk aside them braively.

Anon we came neere the cott, which did look as others in the place. We did open the gaite and Mistress Prue did walk up boldlie to the door and bang on it with her stick. My legges did shake much and my teeth did rattel with feare. Noe anser cummen, Mistress Livvy did say to oppen the door, which Mistress Prue did, I feeling verrie skeert theratt. Noebody saying nay, we all inside; and, la, there was naute to fear, it being onlie a pore gipsie boddie there for shelter, and his wiffe, who was lying sick on sum rubbishy sacks in a corner. Mistress Prue did saye what were they doing, and the man did say they were verrie poore, and no home, and seeing the cott empty they in it one wet night and had stopt there.

HELP FOR THE GIPSIES

I to the pore woman, who did looke verrie ill; to find out that they had no food, onlie what the man did get in the fields of night; and they verrie skeert of bein turned therfrom, did keep quiet. At this we do look to one another, wereuppon I do say can we do anything to help? And the man do say if he can get to his brothers place, he sure of sum work there. But says he, how can he do so with a sicke wiffe? At this I do think quick, and takeing Mistress Prue oute-door do say if we could get her to Sarahs sisters cottage, we could feed her and send her man off about his work, and she later when well. Mistress Prue says the verrie thing to do, if we can without all village knoeing. Going in, we to tell them we will get sum food and help them all we can. They do say God Bless us.

Then we back to Ivy Cottage to arrainge things, and me home, where I did take Sarah to my bedd chamber, and did tell her all, knoeing well she is to be trusted; and did tell her if her sister would look to the pore woman for a while, I would pay her a pennie a day and find her sum food and wood for her fire. Sarah saying she was sure it can be done, I back to Mistress Prue, after telling Sarah to be secrett, taking a basket of bredde, butter, and bakon, as well as a jugge of milk.

Then we to Gunns Cott, verrie braive now we do knowe,

and did tell them what we will do. Then I to Sarah's sister who sayes she will do all she can and glad. So bein settled, tomorrow night we do hope to get the poore retch there in cumfurt.

MAY-DAY CAKES

April ye 30. – Today verrie bussie, and John at work in the forgrounde and not at dinner till late. I did send Sarah home with sum sheetes and a blankit, and divers things reddie for this nights work; then to maken of maye-daye cakes reddie for who shall cum amaying tomorrow, it being maye day. I do make them this way. I do make a paste of white flower and water and butter stiff, and cut in littel roundes, and fill with the following mess. Sum meat and apple and pare chopt very fine, with a bit of union, sum lemmon tyme and a bit of rose-marie, a taste of pepper and salte and a sprinkel of blacke suggar. This I do place in the littel roundes, and wet the edges and turn one side atopp of the other, and presse with hands to make them stick. Then I do beat up a egge and brush over the top and cook in the oven 30 minnetts by the clocke.

A LITTLE WIFELY GUILE

Sarah back to say all be reddie for the pore woman to go, so I do send her to Mistress Prue to tell her I will be at her hous as soon after 6 of the clocke I can. Then me to getting John a good meal for his cumfurt, and thinking it wiser, do think I will tell him. Then I do mix the pigges food all reddie and put the cowes in the byres for the milking. He be pleased, and it did make him fare-minded then. He to a good tee. Me having his pipe all reddie and a good glasse of my eldern-berrie wine, I did tell hym what is agaite, and did make to ask his counsel, not saying oute we had done. He did say not to interfere with them. Then I verrie sly did say it would be

34

verrie kind if he would say Sarahs sister could nurse the pore retch, it being well known he bein a goodly man and kind. To this he did saye verrie well, that he would help us. This pleased me, and I did say to keep it quiet, and not let the village know; to which he agrees, not liking us to be in such cumpanie.

Att nite when all reddie, John and me to Mistress Prue. She bein verrie surprised to see John, I did wisper to her what to do, were uppon she did thank John verrie prettie for his kindenesse for his thought for a poore sowle; so letting him think that he have done all, which did please him, and he did say he would do what he coulde.

Later, when all quiet, wee to Guns Cott, where was Sarah with the poore sowle rapped in a blankit all reddie. John talking to the man, did tell him to starte off; and did give him a silver peece to helpe him with food and drink on the way. To which the man did say the deare lorde would never let him wante. John bidden him carrie his wiffe, we off to Sarah's sister, Sarah in front to warn us if anniboddie about to see us; but did meet onlie a donkie in the church yearde, so get there safe, where Jane had a good fire and the bed warm so the pore sowle soon warme and cumfurtible.

Then I telling Sarah to stope the night, me and John home, after seeing Mistress Prue and her sister safe home; the man cummen with us for sum vittals befor going on to his brother. Then we to bed after barring all the doores and shutters; then I doe rite this wiles John sleepes.

READY FOR CORN-FAGGERS

May ye 2. — Yesterdaye we did have many callers for my maye-daye pyes. So bid Sarah hide sum away in the pig cub-bord for us to ett later. The childer did hav a right ruyall time at the maye pole, and the dansinge did go on merrilie till nigh mid night, when we home to bedd.

*

May ye 6. – Cums Parson Jones to saye no church on Sunday but week night insted. Now there be men cummin for the hay harvest and hoeing, he thinkeing it better so, but John mislikes it

[*At this part of the diary several pages are missing. It continues:*]

June ye 6. – John in to say we must be getting the shed reddie for the corne faggers, now hay harvest be ended. So he do set Old Joe and young Jim to close, and put sum bolterns of straw reddie.

The corn do look verrie well, and wil rippen earlie. It be verrie hot and the cowes did stand in the stream to get cool; and I did oppen the winders, but John did shut them up agen sayen he would get chilled.

Sarah do say my Ladie Susan be at the big hous and do look but poorlie. I do think her visit to London town no good to her.

❧ 6 ❧

ANNE LOSES A GOOD FRIEND

❧

June ye 7. – *and 8.* – Parson Jones in to say church tomorrow night at 6 of the clocke, but I doute if we shall go, being bussie; but shall send Sarah to kepe us in countenance. She do saye to-day she do mislike carters lad, she hearing he do walk with Simpsons lass at the corner when her backes turned. I doe tell her to care for herself, and there be goode fishe in the sea yet; at which she did laff, and say her fishe was heere, and she meant to stay with me.

John hav bin verrie cross at the brindel cow which did knock him over and spil milk on his small cloes. Sarah seeing him did start to giggel, so I did send her to the chest for dry cloes ere John did see her laff, he not liking to be laffed at. But later in the dairy Sarah and me did laff much.

MY LORD MAKES MERRY

June ye 10. – We not to church yester eve, John and me and Sarah bein bussie at cuvvering the hay stackes, now that they be sunk well and wethered. We at it all day between the milking and feeding of pigges and calves; so no tyme to cook, at which John not verrie pleased. Verrie tired, so shall not write annie more now.

June ye 11. – To day me and carters wiffe bussie in the hous, me to the cooking and she to scrubb and clean. At 10 of the clocke she to a food of bread and cheese and cyder. She do tell me that my lord be home at the big house with others as noisie as him selfe. Him be a hartie man and verrie noisie in his cupps. The cook do say to carters wiffe, that my ladie Susan do stop in her own rooms, misliking the rowdie lot and their wayes, and that she be not well, which greeves me. She be a dear ladie and I verrie fond of her, we being together as childer, and she be so kind to all in the place, helping them much.

A FINE CLOAK FOR SARAH

I did get John a good feed by the time he did cum in, and his favvorit pudden of appels, which pleased him. Then he and Sarah to the covvering of the stackes, to finish them. Carter's wiffe do say old Symms at the carpinter shoppe be verrie bad and will die, but he be a man of ripe yeres, and pockitts wel lined for who cums after him.

June ye 13. – I bein so bussie cannot write every day in my

37

booke, but shall do what I can, me liking it much. To-day John did take the woole to sell, and after cleaninge up, me and Sarah to sowing of sum newe shetes, me knowing she be tired after working hard. Later cums my ladie Susan, bringing with her sum more of the chanytee, and a bottel of brandie for John; as well as one off her owne clokes for Sarah. At which Sarah did curtsie, and thank her verrie becoming; then out to sett the bottles reddie for the drinking.

My ladie do look verrie thin and white, and I like not her lookes; but she do assure me she verrie well, but the heat lately trying her much. I fear his lordship do care for noute but his dogges and cuppes. I like not his ruffe wayes. He once trying to kiss me, I did box his eares right soundlie; at which he was so taken abacke, he did walk off rubbing his eares. I must watch Sarah, that she cums not in his waye, she bein a prettie wench.

BAD PRICES FOR WOOL

After tee we to the yardes, me to tell old Joe and Jim to do the feeding; me having my ladie to visit. She did speak verrie prettie to them, and did ask how all did, and did give them a pennie peace; at which they did bless her grately. Then she home, after saying she will cum agen soon, and me to tell John many kind messidges.

Later he home and verrie grumpie, the shepes woole making onlie 9 pence the bagge, which he sayes will not pay him his trubble. He did grumbul at his supper. I did tell him off my ladies visit, and her kind messidges, and did give him sum of the brandie, at which he did cheere up, and was better pleased.

VINEGAR FOR PICKLING

June ye 16. — John cums to say sum of the cyder be sharp and sower, so me and Sarah do get out the vatts and fill with the sower cyder. This we do stand outside, where the sun be hot, and later do put in 2 goode hande fulls of salte, and leve it. In a few dayes we do stir well and leve for another weeke; when we do bring in the vatts of licker and stand by the chimbley corner for another weeke. Then we do straine it clere, and put in a casket and so do we make our vinnegar for the pickellings.

It did thunder much to-day, the lightenen did strike the elm tree by the big gaite, and did kill one of Johns cowes, I fere he will be rathe for dayes, I must feed him well and so hummer him. Men be just like childer and as much trubble in many wayes, but John be a good husban and I would not like to lose him, he bein just a gret babbie for sure.

'HEMPSEEDE I SOWE . . .'

June ye 22. – Laste night after me abed, I did heare a step outeside, and I to the winder; where I did see Sarah off to the stabel yarde. It being 12 of the clocke, I did dress and follow to see whats adoe to the stabel; where she did stop, and me standing by the straw stacke did hear her say: Hempseed I sowe, and he thats my true love cum to me nowe. Then I did see what the sillie wench were doing; she sowing the seed where the carters lad do walk, and his big feet crumping it, the smell there of would reach his nose and so make him to turn to her from all the other wenches. Me knoeing the sillie wench was safe, back to bed; when I did hear her creep in later.

This set me thinking of how I did do the same thing before I did marrie John, me bein sillie likewise. The next day he did ask me to wed, but I did find out later that he did not goe neare where I did strew the hempen seede. So I doute me if Sarahs charme will worke.

*

39

June ye 30. – Newes cums that my ladie Susan be verrie ill with divers doctors to and froe. Carters wiffe do tell me all the visitors be gone, and my lord do set in her room all daye. I be verrie sorrie to hear all this, as is John, who do say to send Sarah to ask how she be, which I do.

ANNE MAKES A HONEY CAKE

She back to say my ladie noe better, the cooke sayeing she be in a high fevver. She do say all the village be stoode at the fronte gaites.

I do pray she may get better, for she be a dere ladie. I did bake bred to daye, and did make a honey cake for Sarah cum her birthday tomorrowe. I do make it this waye. I do take a peese off the bred doe and maken a hole in the middle, I do put in sum furme honey. Then I do neede and patte it, taking care to keep the honey inside. Then I do poke in sum swete plums inside as well as out, then pat it flat aboute a finger thick, and bake it in the oven. When done it be all browne and swete on the top, and makes good etting.

Later we hear there be no better newes of my ladie, she bein verrie ill and the fevver worse; and I do fear for her much. John in to say the faggers will be here in a few dayes, reddie for the corne cutting, so I shall be bussie.

BAD NEWS OF LADIE SUSAN

July ye 2. – Todaye I to the big house to ask how is my ladie, did see my lord; who did look verrie sad and tired, he not bedding this three nights. He did say my dere ladie no better and like to die; at which he did weepe, and I did feel likewise. Poor fellow, he do love her much, in spite of his ruff wayes. I did say I would pray for her recuvvery, and he holding my hand did say, yes pray hard, she be fond of you; which did nearly make me brake down. So I away home, sad indeed, for we hav been frendes all oure lifes, and did play together as childer; albeit she a grate ladie, bless her sweet fase. Sarah was verrie plesed with her birthday cake and Johns mother did send a package for her by Bill Brown, which did reach her todaye; a nice new kercheffe and apron, at which Sarah in loud praise.

The faggers here tomorrowe, so carters wiffe is cumen to cook them sum vittals reddie, and John have put the cyder reddie, for the draweing. I shall be glad when they do go agen, they picken a quarrel often with the villagers.

A SAD DAY FOR ANNE

July ye 3. – This morn did hear the church toll, and did fear much my dere ladie is gone. John cummen in later did tell us she died at 6 of the clocke. It greeves me much, it be a grate loss to me; for I shall miss her sweet fase and loveing wayes. Later cums carters wiffe to work, who do saye my lorde be nerely mad withe greeve, and will not ett, but shut himself up with my ladies boddie and locked the doore. It be sad to dye so younge, she being 24 year olde and her birthdaye the same as mine and the same age. The bell have been tolling all the day. Everie boddie will miss her much, and carters wiffe do say everie boddie is in tears, she being so kind to everie one.

We verrie bussie getting the faggers a meale. John says he will give them all a pennie a day more to get their own vittals, we gives them sum skimm milke and a clene shed to live in. I be verrie glad, for it will save Sarah and me much work, and stopp them bothering at the house at all howers.

July ye 5. – The faggers here last night at 8 of the clocke. They did ett a grate deal, and then to their shed to slepe. There be 4 men and 2 wiffes, pore untidie lookinge trollopes, bet it be a strange life for the pore retches; I fear me I must watch my hen housess and hen nestes.

Todaye did cum a servant from the big house, with a letter from my lord sayeing for me and John to go to the burryinge of my dere ladie; he sayeing she loveing me, he do think she would be wishing it. It do bring teares to my eyes, for indeed I did love her much and shall miss her. So tomorrow me and John to her burrying. This be all I can write; my harte do acke badlie this night.

July ye 6. – To the burrying of Ladie Susan, after telling carters wiffe to cumpanie Sarah cum the time of our returne from the churche; I not lyking Sarah to be alone now the faggers be here.

ᴥ 7 ᴥ

LADY SUSAN'S NECKLACE

ᴥ

[This necklace is still in the possession of the owner of the diary.]

It have rained all the daye, and in the church porch the water did cum drippe drippe from the trees; and I thought me that even the trees did crye for my dere ladies passing. All the village did stand bar headed here to show their respecks but John and me did sett in the church with the mourneres. My lorde did look verrie sadd, and well he might, for he have lost a dele.

Then we oute to the churche yarde agen, where the vaulte had been opened. I could but thinke it be a cold place for her dere boddie to lye till doomesdaye. The bell did toll most drearlie and everie boddie in teares did make all verrie misserible.

After all over, we back home to get into dry thinges; which Sarah had warmeing reddie by the kitchen fire, with a good tot of lemon punche, which we were glad to drinke, it bein such misserable wether. Then John out to see to the works, bidding me and Sarah to stay in the warm kitchen, now there be plentie to do the feeding.

Then me to telling Sarah and carters wiffe of all that had been to do at the church; and they did weep much, and Sarah did show carters wiffe the cloke my dere ladie did bring her less than munthe agon. It be a good cloke, with fur inside it, and Sarah do tressure it.

Then carters wiffe home, me giving her 2 pennies and sum vitles from the larder. Then Sarah and me to soweing and the winding of wool for Johns stockens cum winter.

CARTER'S LAD AND SARAH

July ye 12. – Today hav been verrie hot, and John sayes he be setting the faggers to cutting the wheat cum tomorrowe if it keeps fine as now.

The faggers do make verrie merrie with their songes and fiddelinge, but John do forbidd the village men to cum this yere to cumpanie them. Last yere there was much quarelling. I did see carters lad kiss Sarah at the oute door, so I think he must hav smelled the hemp seed after all. I doute not that the sillie wench will be weddinge him cum later; he be a steddie ladd withal his nonsencie love makeing. One off the faggers wiffes to the house to ask for sackes to cover them at night, there being no door to the shed. Sarah did take her to the barn to get sum, and I did think how better off I be with a good fetther bed to lie on, that was made by my dear mother, of goose down.

I hav got much to be thankful for even if John do be fractious at times; I do feel that God be verrie goode to me and favvoure me much, with a good home and plentie to ett and toe keep mee warm and abel to rede and write.

I be going to teach Sarah next winter, she sayeing she wishe she coulde. She be a goode cooke now, and do not spoil the vittals and verrie clean and tidie. I can trust her alwayes, wherein I be luckie; for Farmer Simpsons maid be a real trollop and not to be trusted like Sarah, who is honnest as the day.

NO RAIN FOR THE APPLES

July ye 15. – We did get noe rain to crissen the appels, so I do hope they will not fall from the trees. For there be a goodely number, as well as pares and plums; also the cob nuts be showing up well.

To-daye did call on me dear ladie Susans mother, bringen a big parssel which she did say for me to have of Ladie Susans cloes; she not wishing them to be put about anniware. And she did also bring me a necklace of redd stones to ware in her memorie, whiche did make me to weep, she wareinge it last time I did see her alive. Her ladieship did ask verrie kind how John did, and did say it was a plessure to cum to so clene a plase; which pleased John mitily when I did tell him later.

Cums carters wiffe with the newes of John Biddels Bess home and to bed with a childe, and she not telling who fathers it. I be verrie sorrie, for they be a tidie pair, and verrie poor, and for their girl to bring shame be a pittye. I do thinke

I will go and see if I can do aught to help them. The whether be so fyne that John do say the wheat can be stacked to-morrow; so we bussie to the bakeings reddie, John likeing to give the men and women sum vittels at after noones with their cyder. Sarah hav made a grett lot of cakes reddie, whiles me to the garden to pick the strawe berries for pickelling and pre-serving. Carters lad did feed the pigges and calves and clene the muck therefrom.

THE FAGGERS QUARREL

Then me in for tee, and later to my bedd chamber to open the parssel off my dear ladies cloes. I did find many things, sum silk gowns and a purpel velvit cloke; as well as sum sweet beddie linen, and night rails.

The necklace I do love much and shall cherish for my own childer when they do cum, so to alwayes keep it in the familie. It do look verrie prettie agon a bright light, and do shine out finely.

July ye 18. – Yester day, John being bussie with the corn stacking, I to Mistress Prue to see if we can do aught for the Biddels. She being sorrie at the news of Bessies downe falle, we to the cott; and telling them we will help if we can, did find they had verrie littel. Me and Mistress Prue home, where I did pack up divers thinges for Mistress Prue to take them, me haven no time to go back for fear of John cummen in. Instead me and Sarah to the wheat ground with sum cakes and 2 jars of cyder; for which they were quite reddie. Then we home to work in the yardes till all done. 2 off the faggers didd start to fight and quarrell, so John payeing them their duties did pack them off, bidding them be gone and nott cum back. I bee sorrie for their wiffes, albeit they did curse at John and say they hoped the rain would cum and spoil all the corne;

45

which I do hope not. I fear me John a bit hastie for now he sayes me and Sarah must help in the harvesting and carters wiffe as well.

MY LORD'S DEPARTURE

July ye 26. – This be the first time for a week I have wrote in my book, bein so bussie working out doores all day; and hard at it when at home, cookeing and such like.

Yester night just when me and John to bed, cums a nocke at the doore; and John to see who is there, did find my lord, who had cum to say goode-bye he bein off to furrin parts, not likeing the big hous with out Ladie Susan.

While he did talk to John, I did get out sum primmy rose wine and cakes to refresshe him. He do seem a altered man nowe and verrie sad to look at in his black cloes; for he do miss my deare ladie sadly.

He did say he was shutting up the big house, but for the servents quarters; and did ask me to look to them sum times which I do promise. Then he did say would I have Nancie, my ladies ponie what she did alwayes ride, for keepes; and I did say yes, albeit feeleing sad to think she not here to ride it. Then he did say for John to hav his brown mare to keep, he not wishing to sell it. John was verrie pleased, and did promisse to car for it, reddie for when me lord back agen. And after talking for divers things, he home agen, telling John to have the fruit from his orchards, and we to go to the hous at annie time. Then bidding me fare well, he did say would I carrie flowers anon to my ladies tomb out of her garden. This do I promise, albeit with tears in my eyes. Then he away, we wishing him godd spede.

8

HARVEST HOME

July ye 31. – Today cum the groom from the big house with Nancie and the browne mare, who did put them in a stabel made reddie for them. Then I taken him to the kitchen for a sup of cyder and sum cake, and we talking, he do say how they do miss my dear ladie; she alwayes so good to one and all, and wanten them to be happie. Then he off back, after sayeing his lordship be off to them furrin partes tomorrowe, and they doute he will never cum backe. John in later to say he been going to stacke the barley, and do want me and Sarah for the lodinge of it to the carter. We were hard at it, to be reddie after dinner. The faggers hav cut all the corne and be off day after tomorrow, so I be giving them a supper for their good work. Sarah and carters wiffe will go in the field the while I do stop home to the cooken.

Aug. ye 3. – John in this morn to say the brindell cow have calved with 2 calves, which he do think be mightily lucky; and later he do bring in a pail of beastlinges, for which I be verrie glad to make puddens for the faggers supper tonight. I do make it like this: I do put the beastlinges in dishes after it is strained, then do shed in sum swete plumms and currents, and a bit of sugger. I shake sum cinnimon over the top, and bake for nearly 2 howers by the clocke. I hav made sum meat pasties and boiled a ham, and baked 3 fowels; and shall bake sum pertaties Johns mothers waye, ands um tartes; they will hav beere and cyder to drink, so they should do verrie well.

Aug. ye 4. – This day me and Sarah verrie bussie baking bread and getting the back kitchen reddie for the faggers supper. Carters wiffe did bring in sum setes for them to sett on, and we did put a tabel in the middle of the flore. John did say it would do verrie well.

At 7 of the clocke they all here, one off them bringing his fiddel; and did give a good look at the good vittals put for them to ett. John did cut up the ham and fowels, giving each a goodlie lot, and they did fall to and ett it up right speedlie; then did set on the pasties and tartes and pudden hartlie. We did watch them the while, John filling up their mugges with cyder and beere as they did empty them.

All fed, carters wiffe and Sarah did clere all oddses from the tabel; and John setting the big jug on the tabel did fetch forth baccy and pipes and did set them easie by saying tune up; when one playing the fiddel, the rest did sing finely. Then John did sing a song, and after I did play upon my spinette; setting the doors open so all could hear; which did please them, they sayeing they had never heard such swete musick before.

STACKING THE CORN

It bein by this time 9 of the clocke, we did give them more to ett and filled up their mugges, and did pay them for their work, and did give each a handful of baccy: while me to the larder to tie up sum odd bittes in a cloth for the women folk to take on their way cum tomorrowe; and did put in their handes a silver peese, unbeknowst to John.

Then they to their shed to sleep to be off yerly next morn. Then John to smoke in the best kitchen the while carters wiffe and Sarah to the clening up to the back kitchen; when she home with the ham bone to pick for her supper and a pastie as well. Now me and John to supper, with Sarah setting with us; and John did give her a glass of eldern berrie wine, for working so hard and well. Then bidden her to go to bed, he did have another tot of the wine, and we to bed also.

Aug. ye 12. – It be over a week since I wrote in my booke, Sarah and me bein harde at it helping with the stackeing of the corn: which be all done now, just in time, for it did start to rain and thunder tonight.

Sarah hav worked verrie hard indeed, so I be going to give her a new gowne, and John a silver peese, he being pleased at the way she do work.

In a day or two we shall be having our harvest home, so we shalle be bussie once more with cooken for a goodlie companie.

Aug. ye 15. – Tomorrow be our harvest home, so todaye Sarah, me and carters wiffe hav been bussie with cooking divers goodies. I did bake 6 bigg fowels that carters wiffe did pluck and draw; and I did cook 3 hares, my dear mothers waye. After taking off their skinnes and pulling out their insides, I did cut them up in peeces, and lay in milk for one hower; while I did chop up 4 apples, 2 unions, a handful of lemmon tyme, sum lemmon rinde, pepper and salt, 3 hard boiled egges, 3 sage leaves and a tee spoon of browne sugger. This be all chopped up together. Then I do put a laire of peeces of hare in a deep dish, then cuvver with the mess. Then a tabel spoon of water, and more hare, and a sprinkel more of the mixed mess till the dish be full. When 3 partes full, I do pore in 2 wine glasse off porte wine. I do then take 4 egges and beat up verrie well with 2 tabel spoone of fresh cream, and a little salte; which I do pore in the dish after the hare hav been cookeing 1 hower and a half; keeping it covvered, ande putting back until the egges be well set. This bee verrie nice cold.

We did boil 2 gret bigg hams and a bakon chine; then there be tartes and custards and other swete things, sum plum

pudden, a chese strait from the vat, and honey cakes and ginger cake. And to drink, sum beere and cyder, sum bottels off brandie, and wines; with milk and lemmon water for the youngsters. There be plenty of baccy, so they shulde do verrie well. Mistress Prue and her sister be cummen, and Parson Jones and his wiffe, Farmer Welles and his wiffe and dauter Monny, and others; also, the work folk and childer, and others from out the village; and Sarahs sister to help.

Aug. ye 17. – Yester eve we did hav a right royal time att oure harveste home partie. Mistress Prue and her sister did cum in the fore noon, to help us get all reddie. We did set the tabels yerlie, and did put green bowes from the box bushes all about the beste kitchen, tied with cullured ribbins; and when done it did look verrie fine.

We did put my spinette in a corner, and the quire did cum with their fiddels for the danceing.

At 6 of the clocke all here, and John did tell all to take their places, the childer setting at a tabel to their selves in the oute kitchen with Sarahs sister to look after them and to see they did hav plenty to ett; whiles the elders did get on with it in the best kitchen.

John did take to top of the tabel, and did carve the hams and baked fowels, while Parson Jones did take the other end and cut up the beefe and bakon chine. And Farmer Welles did fill upp the glasses his side while we ladies did set the other side of the tabel. Johns mother cummen yerlie in the day did serve the bake hare, which everrie boddie did praise grately. Soon mouthes too full to talk till the beer and cyder did losen their tunges; then did they chatter right well. After all had fedd and satisfied inside, Sarah and carters wiffe did start to clere the tabels; which being much to do, me and Mistress

51

Prue, Mistress Jones and Johns mother did help to put the dishes in the dairies for safetie.

THEN TO DANCING

Then back to find the men folk had put the tabels agen the walls, and the fiddels tuning up for a danse; to which we did all futt it right merrelie. The childer did hav a good time albeit overfull from their good feeding.

Then we did set down the while the men did drink beere and cyder, and the ladies each a glass of wine, eldernberrie or primmy rose, which they fansied.

Carter now did stand up and sing a hunten song, every boddie helping in the chorous at the top of their voices. Shepperd and his wiffe did sing a song of the poacher, and divers others likewise. Then Mistress Prue did play olde tunes on my spinette, as did me also; the childer gathering round. Mistress Prue did make them sing a harvest himn, which she did play on the spinette for them, and which they sung finely. Then to danceing agen. Old Granfer Tollu did ask me to trip a messure with him, which I did, and right well for all he be 80 cum next marche. Then more singing and so on, till at last everrie boddie did set them selfes downe with the pipes and glasses to tell tales.

LOUD CHEERS FOR ANNE

Olde Granfer did tell us of a goste what did walk everie satterdaye night past the beech tree road, who turned out to be a old gray goate. At this we did laffe, and ole granfer was so excited he did set down with a bump on the floor; and I did give him a glass of primmy rose wine to take the hurt from his back-sete, and did tell him to set in Johns arm chair.

So did we plessure oure selfes till nigh mid nighte. Then

the tabels layed open, all did fall to, and after Parson Jones upp and says the health of the ladies, gentelmen; which they did drink hartily. Then we do drink to the men. Then John did say drink to those who had worked to give them a good supper. This they did agen and agen, till Johns mother did bring forrard Sarah and me and carters wiffe in front of all, and did say 3 chere for us, which they did right hartily. Then once more passing the jug and bottels round, more talk and cheering; till all holding hands we did sing to our next meeting. At length they home, right full and merrie; and then me, carters wiffe, Sarah and Johns mother to the dairie to wash the dishes, which were mannie.

Mistress Prue and her sister did help to wash the glasse; they stopping to sleep with us. Then to the tyding off the kitchens reddie for the morne.

A GOOD HEALING DRAUGHT

Aug. ye 20. – This be the first time I hav writ in my book for three dayes, bein bussie.

It hav bin a verrie hot day and we to church at night, after the milking be don and the pigges fed.

The passon was new, and did preche a verrie prosie surmon, so I nearly aslepe, and did jump much at the last himm singeing. I was glad to be out once more, and John bidden the passon to supp with us we back home, where Sarah cumming in, we did put the supper reddie in the best kitchen.

Aug. ye 21. – Up yester morn att 4 off the clocke, and carters wiffe cumming we to the washing; getting all reddie for the hangeing out before breakefuste.

John in to saye Dollie the red cow be sicke, so me to make a drink for her good, it bein chill. I do warme sum milk, to which I do put a spoon full of breesed appel pips and 2 egges, all shook upp with a glass of brandie, which John do give her. Later she much better, and John did give her milk to the calfs.

Carters wiffe do say Emma Tranter hav got an arm broke through falling from off their tallett steppes; and that Farmer Joneses Marye be getting wed to Bill Somers, at which I be not surprised, hearing a whisper anon. But I doute me if they hav got much to start on, the old Jones be farelie warm, so folkes do say.

TWO SHEEP LOST

Later John cum in to say Farmer Ellis be cum, lookeing for 2 sheep which he hav lost, and much fears they be stol. Wher on carters wiffe do up and say she did see two strange men in the village yester eve; which be verrie odd to my thinkinge, as I do say to Farmer Ellis when I out to the gate with a tot of cyder for him. And he agrees, so he be off to the squire to see about it; and I back to the kitchen feeling verrie sorrie for the poor wretches if they hav done the stealing, for it be a serious thing to steal a shepe.

9

OUTCRY ABOUT SHEEP-STEALING

❧

Aug. ye 23. – Me and Sarah bein bussie with lime washen of the kitchen and house place, John hav to feed the pigges and calfs, which do fuss him much; and the big boar pigg biting him hard on the leg, he cums in most wrotheful, and sayes he will hav us out cum tomorrow. At which I do say how can we when we so bussie? So he off out agen after hitting the cat with my pewter pepper pot.

Then in cums Sarah with her hand all bloddie, and she crieing, saying she did do it with the big carver. This I do wash and tye with a peece of old shirt.

John in agen do say whats ado, and me telling him, he mighty cross, saying it be all done apurpus to vex him and not to go out to help him. Indeed he be verrie wrothe.

JOHN OVERHEARS . . .

At this I be so cross I uppes and sayes Sarah be my maid not his, and he to get out of my kitchen till his temper be better. So he out, shutting the door with a grate noise, saying that wimmen was the verrie divvell; at which I so wrothe I did throw a lump of bredd at him, but only hit the shut doore. Then I did pictur to myself Johns face if I had hit him, and fell to laffing so hartilie that the tears did run adown my cheekes. John do think he be such a grett man, but lord he be just a bigge sillie.

Then me telling Sarah all, she do say: make him a pan cake, and he soone better. So she off to bring sum egges warm from the neste, and we set to makeing agen John do cum in.

55

I did also get out a bottle of my fuzzy [furse or gorse] wine, this bein a grate favourit of his.

Now Sarah who be a sensie maid do say, here he cums; and do start to say how happie she be to be living with us and what a good master John is, and her plase here so much better and higher up than anie other farmers place anie ware, and he as good looking gentleman as anie here.

I do look at John from my eye corner and sense he lookes verrie pleased, not knowing it be all apurpus. Then he inside to say give him the paile for to fetch in the egges, which Sarah does.

TWO MEN IN JAIL

Later we to supper, and John etting his bellie full do say the fuzzy wine be grand, and to give Sarah a tott; she being a good wench and respectful to her betters. This I do, and Sarah did thank him verrie prettie, and wishing him good luck did drunke it uppe.

Aug. ye 25. – Cums John in to say that the aftermuth crop of clover in the lowe meddowe be fit for the cutting, and he will want me and Sarah as well as carters wiffe to help. Wereon Sarah do say her sister Jane would be glad to help, not haveing much to do all day. To this John agrees, and Sarah home and back with Jane.

So after sum food and a drink of cyder we to the lowe meddow, where all bussie.

Carters wiffe do cum to me to say had I heard the newes, to which I sayes no, what is it? Then she do say that the 2 men be had that they think did steale Farmer Ellises shepe, but they sayes they knowe naught about any shepe, being new-cummers but 3 days before at the old Mill Cott. But they be in the jail hous safe and sound.

At this I do say, be there a wiffe or childer? To which

carters wiffe do say one of them hav got a wiffe and 6 childer. Wereon I do feel verrie sorry, and do say so.

John now cumming to us do ask be we going to cabbel all day and do naught? So we work with the rest, till time to go to the pig-feeding; which I do, to leave Sarah hard at it.

Later cums Mistress Prue to tell me of a new pudden which she did make, and with a bitt for me to taist. Me liking it much, she do tell me how to do it.

You do peel sum pares and cut them up in 4 peaces to each pare, then put sum peaces of bred and butter in the bottom of a deep dish, and lay the pares on top. Then more bred and butter, throwing on sum sugger and a pinch of cynamon. Then you do take 4 egges and beat them hard for a bit, then put them in a measure of milke and beat up till frothie. Now pour over the pudding in the dish and cook it gentlie for a hower by the clocke. I shall do it for John later, but fear I must mayke a big one for him, he bein a hartie etter, much to his discumfurt some wiles. After a dish of tee I do ask Mistress Prue if she do know ought of the poor wretch of a wiffe at Old Mill Cott, saying I do feel sorrie. She agrees, and did say she will go herself and see if they do need vittals. And I did tell her to let me know, and I will help, albeit quietly. Then she off, and I to the milking and feeding of the calfes.

AN UNPOPULAR SERMON

Later Sarah in to say the master be cumming for his tee, and she off to get reddie. John cumming, I do tell him how the men be jailed, and he sayes it be a good thinge too; so I not say I be sorrie, or that Mistress Prue be going to see what ado. But I did say she did call to see me. Then he out to see all is well in the stocke yardes, and me up to my bed chamber to write this in my booke.

*

Aug. ye 27. – We verry bussie with the cooking and cleaning yesterday, so did not write in my booke, for we must be all-wayes reddie for any boddie who do call.

We to church this morne, and John did fidgett much, he not liking thee passon; which be a new one, who did tell us that hell be nere and we all going there; and that it be wronge to heard monies, for the divell will get it all. Ande he did look

so hard at John that I did fear he off from the church wrothe-fullie. But John did staire back at the man, and fould his armes and look puffed up. Then we out, and meeting in with Farmer Ellis and his wiffe, we did carrie them off with us; also Mistress Prue and her sister. Back home to find Sarah had got the dinner reddie and the tabel lookeing very fine with my glass and silver laid upon it, which we do alwayes hav now, John thinkeing we can well afford to do as the qualitie do.

It bein a verrie hot day, we ladies do not ett so much, but the 2 men did set to right hartilie and made gret inrode on the beefe rounde.

Then Sarah did cum for her plate full and John do alwayes put plentie.

Then me and she do clere all away, and her sister Jane cummin I do leeve them to the washing of the dishes and to tidie the hous place: and we to the best parlour, leaving the men to their cyder. Later we all out to look at the pigges and other cattel in the yardes.

HELP FOR THE CHILDREN

Farmer Ellis do say he be sure the 2 men be the right ones, what had his shepe; and he thinkes they should be hung for it. At which I do look at Mistress Prue, not knowing if she have seen the poor wiffe as yet.

Later Farmer Ellis and his mistress home for the milkeing, and John also. We back to the hous, and right glad to be out of the hot sun.

And then Mistress Prue do say she and her sister Livvy had bin to the old Mill Cott, to see the shepe steelers wiffe; and they find all clene, but the children verrie hungrey and etting raw turmot toppes. At this I say how can we send them sumthing to ett? John will not saye do, if I did ask, so I must say naught to him. Then I do think that Sarah will help and so called her in, and telling her we did trust her much I did say could she carrie a baskit to Mistress Prue? And she sayes anything she can do to help she will and say nought. So Mistress Prue after praising her did say go sumtime tomorrow.

We do puzzle what best to do, then sayes Sarah we be going to stack the clovver earlie tomorrow, and the master bussie then, see she can get off later; wereon we do say let it lie, and Sarah to take a baskit furst chance. Then she out to the kitchen to boil the kettle for the tee drinking and we out to the yardes to bring in the egges. The hens be laying well now, but the egges be verrie chepe, being 3 pence for 30; but I be thankfull I can still add to my stocking, having now a goode sum for my own.

After tee drinking, we out and did walk to the clovver grounds; and John sayes it must be in the stack cum tomorrow night.

STACKING THE CLOVER

We hard at it by earlie morn, then we to Ivy Cott with Mistress Prue and her sister for sum supper, then we home to bed to be reddie for the mornes work betimes.

Aug. ye 29. — Yesterdaye we up at 4 of the clocke, and to the meddowe for the stackeing of the clovver hay, the dew on it being just right for the stackeing. After that finished, me and Sarah home to the cookeing of dinner. By the time John do cum, he be better tempered than of late because of the good crop of clovver.

After he off agen, Sarah sayes should she go to Ivy Cott with the baskitt of vittals for the pore wretches; she sayeing John away, this is our chance. So me to the packeing of sum oddses; a peece of fat baken, sum butter and a duzzen of egges; as well as a big lofe of bred of my own bakeing, and a lump of cheese, and a silver shillen – bein sorrie that the wiffe and childer should suffer for no faulte of their own. Then Sarah away, and me to the mixing of the pigges vittals and the calfes, reddie for the feeding later. And after did tidie the strawe yardes, putting all verrie clene genst John cumming home.

❧ 10 ❧

MISTRESS JONES ASKS A FEW QUESTIONS

❧

Sept. ye 1. – To-day I have been verrie bussie with the baking of bred and pies, and I did make the pudden Mistress Prue did bring me to taiste. John praised it much, and did clene out the dish, me having a littel peece; but it was verrie good and a nice change.

After me and Sarah to the clening out of the pigges, a verrie muckie job, and later cums Sarah with a hen she did find killed by a foxe; which vexed me much, it bein one of the best layers. So I the poorer. I did tell her to take it home to her sister to make broth for the childer, and me say nought to John, he not likeing to lose annie thing.

After tee cums carters wiffe to say that Farmer Ellises shepe be found at a stone quarry about 2 miles from here, all safe and sound; and that the 2 men be let go, for which I be verrie glad. She did say that Ann Tranters washing did look verrie dirtie on her wash line, but she been feckless boddie and verrie untidy. Her face do alwayes be looking in need of a wash bowl.

BUT NO WORK FOR THEM

Carters wiffe did say that Farmer Jones be verrie jellus of John, and that in the Crowne publick he did say John be got verrie uppish of late, and that he did not think we had got much. At which I did say he would have more of his own if he did keep away from the Crowne and look to his wayes; to which carters wiffe do say the master be not uppish, but quite a fine man, to which I do hartilie agree.

Later did cum a nocke on the door, it bein the 2 men for a job of work now they be out of jail. I feared much they would say about the baskett of oddses, but all they did want was a jobbe of work. But John said now he hav plentie of men. So after drinking sum cyder, and etting sum bred and chese, they off and we to bed, it being 9 of the clocke and late.

A PINCH OF CHINA TEA

Sept. ye 3. - We not to church this day, John sayeing it be Passon Ellis, and not likeing him or his wiffe we stay away. After dinner John to slepe in the best parlour while me and

Sarah to the washeing of dishes, and tydieing of the house place. Then Sarah home till 7 of the clocke, and me and John to the feeding of the pigges and calfes; and Tim to the milkeing, he bein a useful lad and works well.

Later cums Farmer Jones and his wiffe to talk with us, and we in to stay drinkeing which Sarah hav put all reddie before going home. John and Farmer Jones do drink beer with their platters of ham, but me and Mistress Jones do drink sum of my Chiny tay, that my dear lady did give me; I still having sum left.

She never taisting it before, did praise it highly; so that I did give her a pinshe, albeit onlie a pinshe.

After, we to talkeing, and she tells me that Bella Griffin be cum home from her plase, and had bin to her for work in the house or on the land, but sayes Mistress Jones, Bella not lookeing verrie clene or tidie, she did say no. Then we fell talkeing of my dear lady, she telling me folkes do say I did hav much munnie when she died, but that we say nought. So I do tumbel to the reason of their visit, it bein onlie to find out for sure.

So I verrie warie, and say but littel, but I did let her look at my necklace and a velvitt cloake, at which she did say how good it was and she did envie me the necklace. But, sayes she, I was the one to carrie it off well; to which I did agree.

Then we down the stayers, to hear Farmer Jones say they must be off; he to see a calfing cowe. So we did walk a peese with them to look at the shepe on our way back.

Then John did say, did she say ought of my Lady? And I did tell him what she did say. Then he tell me Farmer Jones did say much the same to him, but that he did say nought; but to let him find out, it bein our business.

But I like not our nayburs to be jellus of us. John says they will sonne tire if we say nought, and I hartilie hope so.

Sarah cums in earlie and lookeing mitie glumm, and speake-
ing but littel. I fere me there be trubble againe. After supper
we toe bed earlie, reddie for the butter makeing and washeing
cum thee morn.

Sept. ye 5. – We up earlie yester morn and Carters wiffe here
by 5 off the clocke. She to the washeing. John and Sarah to
the yardes, the while I do cook the breakfast agen they be
reddie; with a gret platter full for Carters wiffe in the back
house. John sayeing fat lambes be makeing a good price, he
off with sum to markett; and me to the butter makeing. After
a bussie morn, we reddie for our meale betimes; carters wiffe
setting with me and Sarah, much to her delight, she sayeing
that when she do go to Farmer Joneses to help with the
washeing, they do put her a rabbitts jimmie and naught else
but taties and a cup of cider, in the wash hous; and do pay her
but 2 pense for her dayes work. Wereby she sayes she will
always cum to me first, seeing that her platter be always as
good as my ownn and well payed for what she does. This be
trew, me paying her 4 pense a day and withe oddses to her
baskiett.

Sarah bein verrie strange and not speaking, I do think I
will ask later what is afute.

CARTER'S LAD AND BELLA

Then other divers jobbes, till in cums carters wiffe to say the
pigges be fedd and she off agen to the cows milkeing; Sarah
to feed the calfs and hens. Then they in later for their tee,
and carters wiffe home with sum oddses for her supper from
my cubbord.

Then I do say to Sarah what is the matter with her all day,
at which she do start to howl, ande I do say, what is it? And

after her howleing a bit she do say carters lad be walkeing out with Bella Griffin, and did pass her by and not look at her; but that Bella did giggle at her in passeing; and that she do hate carters lad, and do hope he will be off for a soljer out of her way. At this I do tell her to drie her teares, and let him go his gaite, and take no more notice of him. Then Sarah did say he be welcum to Bella, for all she did care. Then, said I, what was she crying for, like a pigge? And that I was ashamed of her howleing, there being plentie of lads to go acourteing. At which she sayes she do hate men, and a pittie they be borne at all; wimmen bein so much the kinder; at which I do laff and she dries her teeres, and to work. But I`will talk to Carters lad later, not likeing Sarah to be sorried so.

.

A YOUNG PARSON VISITS THE HUGHES

❧

John in later from the market, and not verrie plesed; getting onlie a poor price for the fat lambes. He thinks it be oweing to folks thinking us better off than we be. So I did give him a tot of brandie and after that he much better tempered; and do say we must pick the appels cum to morrow, reddie for the cider makeing.

And so we to my lordes orchard, to see if the appels be reddie for the picken, as is our owne; and to the big house to tell the caretaker to have the 2 big caskes reddie cum the morn, for carter to fetch for the filleing; John sayeing it be onlie fair they should hav sum for their drinking. We shall hav the appels good for the cookeing for oure selfes. Later we to the carters cot to tell carters wiffe to be reddie betimes for

65

the picken cum morn; then we home and to bed. We did see carters lad and Bella Griffin standeing beside a gaite as we did cum home, a-giggling; which did make me verrie wrothe, so that I did eye them verrie severe in passing.

CARTER'S BOY AND BELLA

Sept. ye 8. – Hav bin bussie with the appel picken this 2 dayes, and there be now grate store; so John thinkes he will press all cum tomorrow. So Shepherd and Jim and old Joe did clene the press and get all reddie, while Sarah and me to the cooking of much food reddie for the men; and our own reddie for over the sabbothe.

Yester day I did question carters wiffe about her lad and Bella Griffin, and she did say she be main vexet at his treating Sarah so, but what can she do? Wereon I do say I will talk to him sharpe, but that I think Sarah well rid of him. Later John to Mistress Prue with a bussell of our best cookers, as he do everie yere; she with no orchard of her own. Then did cum a letter to ask John to entertain the passon cum Sunday; he cumming here by 6 off the clocke on Satterday, and he to slepe with us. I did tell John it will make much harde work for me and Sarah, so he did say tell Carters wiffe to cum and help; which I had alreddie done, albeit letting John think he is the clever one.

I doute if I shall write in my book for a while, being bussie with the cider makeing, and getting reddie for the passon cumming.

A YOUNG LAD, THE PARSON

Sept. ye 9. – John cums in to say he will let the cider makeing stop till Tewesday, now that passon be cumming. I be verrie glad to hear this. Bein bussie I cannot write more in my book but we to bed.

*

Sept. ye 13. – The new passon cum on Saterday; a young lad of 20 yeres or so. I be glad we did do much cookeing for he did ett much, being clemmed of his journie.

We to church on the Sabboth, and did heare a plessent sermon. John did nod as alwayes, but the passon did pleese me much, for he did not tell us that the divvel would hav us for caring for sum monies, but did say the world be a verrie good plase to live in; and be good to the poore, was the true religun. To which I do hartilie agree.

Then we home to dinner, carrying off Mistress Prue ande her sister Livvie; where we did find Sarah had put all reddie. We did have roste goose stuffed with boiled egges and sweete appels, which did cum out nice and jouisey; sum shepe mutton, and 2 roste hens; a round of befe boiled, and taties and soe on – as well as a mylke pudden, and a appel and divers others. To which all did do justis, and Mistress Prue praising Sarahs cookeing much, did pleese me. And I did see passon look at Sarah verrie prettie. After dinner John and passon out to see sum of the village folke, to see how they do; which be verrie nice of him, being the firste passon I ever knowed to do so.

HIS GHOST

Then we ladies to talking of divers thinges, the wile carter's wiffe and Sarah do ett their dinner and later wash the dishes. Mistress Prue did say as how the talk was that carter's ladd was wedding Bella, and sayes she, what did Sarah saye? To which I uppes and sayes Sarah had more sense than to bother herself about him, and Mistress Prue agrees, sayeing she be worthie of a better man, bein a prettie maid and daintie in her wayes. To which I accord hartilie.

Then Mistress Livvy did saye that she did see old Amos Court's ghoste in his orchard cum dark tother night, as he were on his waye home from the Crowne. It be verrie strange, but he do allus cum at cider-makeinge every yere since he died. But he were a bad old man and so do not rest; as Mistress Prue did saye, he be still harkeing after other folkes appels and pares. For he did used to rob folkeses orchards and sell cider to his gaine. I hope he will not cum to our orchards, for I like not the thought of a ghoste.

WHERE IS THE HOUSE?

Mistress Prue did laff and say, how can a ghoste pick appels? Albeit divers folkes do say they be picked, and old Tom Tranter do say he did hear a carte bump in his orchard and old Amos telling the horse to wowe; but I dout me if it be trew, for old Tom could allus tell a good lie strait out. Later John and passon back, and they to talkeing that it be likelie we to have a passon to live in the village; and John to call a metting of divers folkes to talk about it. But, sayes Mistress Livvie, there be no house. John, looking verrie wise, do say he is not so sure about that; at which they fall to askeing him for more. But he will say nought. Then Sarah in with the tee pot and we fell to, it being 4 of the clocke and 2 howers sence we last fed. Passon did look at Sarah much and I did think they would make a hansum paire. He be a nice lad.

Mistress Prue did ask him how he would like to be our passon for good, to which he say how good John and me had bin; and he would like much to live here, we all so kind to him. To which Mistress Prue did say he might be where he will be well cared for if with me and John. At which John did make her a fine bowe, and did thanke her, sayeing he must not contradickt a ladye; at which did all laff.

Later we to church, which did fill right up, everie boddie wishing to see what the newe passon be like. I did see carter's lad and Bella setting by the door, and they did staire much to see Sarah setting by my side like a ladye. I did look verrie hard at them both, wereon they both looked shippishe. Betsie Ann Arthers from Hollowe grounde had got on another new bonnit, but I doute if it be paide for; she having so many, and onlie verrie little monies. A feckless boddie she be. We home anon to supper. It was verrie hot, and verrie plessant to be back in my nice kitchen.

HANDSHAKE FOR SARAH

Sept. ye 15. — We hav made much cider these 2 dayes, and John cum in to say old Joe had got a bellie ake with too much drinkeing of the newe jouice. But I pittie him not, he being a greedie olde man who do want all.

Passon did go away on Mon-morne, after thankeing me and John right hartilie. He did aske much about Sarah, and I feare me he will want to cum acourten her. He shaiken her by the hand, she did go verrie pink, the sillie wenche.

John in later to say the meeting about the new passon's hous bee here this nighte at 7 off the clocke, so Sarah and me to the boiling of a stuft ham in reddinesse; and other thinges. Folkes do like my stuft ham, and I do them thus. I do set the ham on its back, and take out the bone, then I do fill the hole all down the middle with this mess: 4 choppt appels, 2 choppt unnions, a bigg spoon full of choppt sage, a cup of choppt parslie, and 2 big hande fulle of bredd rubbed small; and sum salt and pepper to flavour it. Then I do pour over all 6 egges beat to a frothieness, and this I do throw overall and mix up well, and put it in the ham hole. Then I do tie it verrie tight in a clene cloth, and boil about 4 howers, and not take off the cloth till verrie cold.

The stuffen do cut out with the meat verrie well. This be a nice dish and swete etting.

We shall put it in the sellar to get cold, which it soon does if put agen a full beer cask.

They do say that the ghost of old Amos be picken all the appels off John Buttell's trees, he findeing them all gon yester morn when he do go to his orchard. But I must write no more now, it being time for the milkeing.

꽃 12 꽃

THE COUNTRYSIDE GOES TO A WEDDING

꽃

Sept. ye 17. – We did hav divers folkes here to the meeting for the passon's hous. Farmer Bliss did say its verrie well, but where the hous? Whereone the butler from the big hous did say that my lord did offer Gunns Cott, and he to make all tidie, if John thinks propper; and sum chaires and ettcettera for the passon's use.

Then Mistress Prue did offer a bed and 2 chaires, and others offering, John will make up the reste from my lordes big hous. So it be settled, and John sayeing he did like much the young passon, they all say yes, he must cum. I be verrie glad for he is a nice lad.

I did talk to carters lad toe-daye, and did rate him soundlie for his bad treateing of Sarah, and giveing him a gret boxe of the eers, which did make him youpe, and bidden him to cum no more to the hous on paine of a horse whippen. I did make him worke verrie harde at divers jobbes till he verrie glad when time for home did cum. I fear me if the new passon do cum to live here, he will wante my Sarah, bein verrie strucke with her as I could see. But I shall not stand in her way. She be a good maid and I like her much.

Sept. ye 19. – Carters wiffe cums for the scrubbing of the passidges and to the lime washeing of the dairy; and do tell me that old Tranter did go home in a woefull frite yester-night, sayeing that he cumming home at after dark did meet old Amos Courts ghoste; with a gret bigge black dogge, with eyes like saussers which did shoot fire. And that old Amos did grone much and did hit old Tranter with a gret bigge appel so that he hurt sum what. Carters wiffe do say she be skert to go nigh a orchard for fere of Old Amos, but I dout if old Tranters tale be true, knowing well his lying tongue. But I like not the talke of ghostes and such things. Mistress Prue cumming for her butter, I do tell her; at which she do laff hartilie, and do tell me not to caddel myself; that there be no such things as ghostes. So I do laff with her, albeit not feeling verrie sure.

Carters wiffe did say that Betsie Ann Arthers be in danger of lossinge her home threw bein sold up fur debte; she bein a verrie spendie wretch, and do save naught, yet do put on new gownes and bonnits, and so do waste her monies what she should put in her stockinge.

Sept. ye 21. – Cum a man with a letter to say will we go to his dauter's wedding cum next Munday; and that Mary do wante Sarah, to be her maid. This I tell Sarah, who do saye, will I agree? To which I did, and did tell her I will dress her myself; at which she verrie pleesed.

Me telling the man to say Master Hughes and me will go if possibel, he off, after drinking a cup of cider and etting a lump of bred and ham.

So it do seem young Somers be wedding Mary after all. Butt I fere there will be verrie littel to start with. John in, I do tell him of the wedding, and what I did say back; and he quite reddie, if nothing ado to hinder. And so its setteld. Later cum Farmer Jones to say the young passon will do for Mary. John do saye he agree, so all be reddie.

SARAH DRESSES UP

Farmer Jones gone, John and me to talking what best to give Mary for a present, and John saying that the little blacke sowes pigges be reddie for the weening, he will give her 3, and what will I doe? Then I do saye she can hav one of my linnen tabel clothes; to which John agrees. Then we out to the pigge feedeing, and later Sarah and me to the pressing of the clene clothes and aireinge it to put away, reddie to use.

Sept. ye 24. – Bein bussie, I hav no time to write in my book till now. John bein gone to the smithes shoppe, me to my littel booke.

The new passon be here for the wedding cum to-morrowe, and be gone out with John. His name be Godfrey Cross, a verrie prettie name. I fere me much that he be struck with Sarah, but hope not, for I wish not to lose a good maid.

After dinner she and me to my bedd chamber, to see for her gowne out of the big cheste. Me takeing a prettie gowne of white silk with pink roses upon it, did bid her put it on; which she did, turneing about and about for me to see. She looked verrie fine. Then I did out with sum shoes with silver buckells, and a bonnitt of pink straw with white roses under, to set on the haire. She putting all on, did look rarelie; and so pleesed was I that I did carry her to the best kitchen for John and passon to see. They did praise her mitilie, and I could see passon was verrie struck at such a prettie wench. Then we back up stayers agen to put away the finerie till to-morrowe, and Sarah did say with teares in her eyes how she did wish her mother could see her in her prettie cloes. I did say, howe

good it would be; for I did know just how she did feel; for many a time I hav wished my own deer mother was here to see and hear this and that.

So after cumferting Sarah, we back to tee drinking; and me askeing John first, did bid Sarah to set at our tabel. Passon be slepeing here to night in the best bed chamber, on a verrie good fether bed my dear mother did make from her goose fethers.

Sept. ye 26. – Yester morn we up betime to be reddie for Mary Jones weddinge att 11 of the clocke. The sun didd shine and it were verrie warm. Carters wiffe cumming to help in good time we finish work erlie.

Then mee and Sarah upp to her bedd chamber, after me putting reddie Johns best velvet britches and blue silk stocke-ings with the purpel plusshe coate of my lordes with the gold lace, and his best shoes with two big golden buckles, and his best hat. Carters wiffe did praise Sarah much sayeing that she never in her born days did see such a daintie maid in all her finerie. Then I to my bedd chamber to put on my blue silk gown with the wide lace flounces of butter cullor; and shoes with the glass buckels, which were my dear ladies; and a blue straw bonnitt with the white ribbons; and did wear my red necklace which did look verrie fine.

Then me to help John into his britches, which he did get in to after much puffing and grunting; but indeed I was verrie proud when all reddie; and John, mighty proud to see me and Sarah lookeing so fine, did bid Carters wiffe to have a care not to over feed the black sowe and to be sure to strip the cows of all their milk. We off to the church in good time, John mighty proud to be in the cumpany of 2 such fine ladies, he did say, laffing at us.

Then mee not knowing if I had locked up the meat safe in the dairy, was about to turn about; but Sarah telling me she had done it herself, and put away turkey in the brown pot, I more content and into church, where were all the folk reddie who did stare at us with mouth agape as we did get to our seats; Sarah stopping with us till the wedding partie did cum. Mary did look verrie cumlie in her white gown with a fine lace kerchief; but my Sarah did out shine them all with her dark curlie hair and prettie pinke cheeks. A wedding be a verrie sollum thing, and not to be entered into lightlie; one do make sum verrie grate promisses which we must keep and not fail therein. I could not help but think how blest I was with my John at my side; albeit he be like a great baby at times with his show of temper. I did feel the dear God had bin good to me and my own life had fell in plessente places. The passon did read the service verrie well, and did give a good exortashun to end all. Then we all out and to the Ley Farm where we did find all reddie, so every body falling to did make a good meale; then John as becum the biggest farmer did say let us drink the brides helthe which every body did with much laffing at her blushes; then up gets Farmer Lewis from Blackmores to say lets drink to the 2 prettiest ladies in the place – Mistress Hughes and her maid Sarah; long life to both, at which I did stand up and say my thanks and say that Sarah was as good a maid as she was prettie, at which they did all shout agreement and fill their glasses.

FIDDLERS STRIKE UP

John was mighty pleased at all this; then old Timothy Martin did say if he was 50 years younger he should cum acourten Sarah, at which all did laffe and she blussh as red as a cherrie;

but I did like her manners much, she being verrie modest and not putting her self forrad at all.

Then the fiddelers strikeing up a lively tune we to danceing rite reddie, after so much jigging about.

There were many cakes and divers things, but not baked to my mind a bit, me lykeing them verrie light, not lumpie. Later cum Mary and her man to thank me and John for our presents which did please them both. Then we home not stopping for more danceing; and Sarah and the passon cuming with us, John did wispur that it would be a good thing for Sarah, and a step up to be a passons wife. Att which I did tell him to stop it, me not wanting to lose Sarah; but I do see they be mighty good friends. We home to find all work done and Carters wiffe reddie for home, but I did bid her stop a while, knoweing she did want to hear all. So we to drink a cup of tea, and me telling her all about the wedding and giveing her 3 little cakes Mistress Jones had give Sarah for her. She was mighty pleased, and did say she sure no boddie did look finer than we, and that the master didd look as good a gentelman as my lord hiselfe; and she be right for John did look verrie fine in deed.

Then she home and me and Sarah up stairs to take off our finery. I did tell Sarah to put away her gown and hat and shoes in her own chest and to keep it for her own at which she did

thank me verrie prettie and did put it over the bed rail to air, before putting it away. Then I to my chamber likewise to change clothes and down again, did go to the yards to see all well; then me and John and Passon did go to Gunns Cott to see how it does. It do look much nicer now and men be putting on a new roof; and John do say it must be called the passenage now. Then we home to supper which Sarah had all reddie for us, and to bed.

Sept. ye 28. – Yesterday we to the washeing and butter makeing. Carters wiffe here at 5 of the clock, we soon get all done and then to the makeing of pies and cakes; and also the makeing of a honey cake, bein Johns favourit cake.

HONEY-CAKE AND ROLLIES

I do make it thus: A lump of butter, a bigg cup of sugar, 3 eggs, a messure of swete plums, a messure of flour, and sum milk. I do beet the eggs and butter and sugar with a cup of honey till it be verrie frothie and bubbelie; then I do put in the flour and beet it again till verrie light, then I do throw in the swete plums and put all in a greased pan and bake in the bredd oven till it be cooked. This be a verrie prettie cake.

I did also make sum rollies, which be made by putting sum flour in a bowl then drop in 4 eggs and a bit of sugar and beet it up to a soft mess, then put in a long tin and bake gentlie. When it be cooked, I do turn it out gently on a board and put on sum swete plums and nut-meg and sprinkel with sugar, then roll it up and put away till cold.

JOHN BURNS HIS FINGERS

Later there came a poor boddie for sum bread to eat, a poor traipse of a woman with her clothes in rags and no shoes. I did give her a lump of bread and chesse and a cup of cider; she did ask for work, but I could not have a traipse about, and did say so. So she off for which I was verrie glad, not wishing John to think I do encourrage such; but I do always feel sorrie for them, me bein so much the better off. Then John cums in to say we must take the honey from the bees so he to the makeing of sulfur papers, which he do put near the fire. It flaring up, did burn his fingers: thereby he did drop all on my clene harthe stone, and did dance about like a bee in a bottel. I was verrie wroth at my harthe bein all messie, and did say it did serve him right for being such a great sillie. Weron he did say it be all our folte and to be plagued with a passel of women be enough to try any man.

I did put sum butter on his finger to stop the smarten theron, but he did make a mighty fuss. Sarah did scrape up the sulfur from the harthe stone and clene it, but it be stained and do smell verrie nastie; and I did tell John not to do it in my clene kitchen agen but in the washe hous, and did take all ther, bein crosse at the waste of good sulfur. Later Carters wiffe did cum and make a goodlie pile of the papers, and so we now all reddie to take the honey on to morrow.

Sept. ye 30. – We did have a bussie time takeing the honey from the bees yester night. Me and Sarah and Carters wiffe did have to do it all; John sayeing his fingers bein verrie sore from the burnes.

Sarah did dig a big hole in the ground for each skeppe, where in we put a sulfur paper which we did set alight, and put the skeppes of bees on the topp. The smell of the sulfur do kill the bees, and so we do get the honey therfrom.

It do grief me to kill the poor things, bein such a waste of good bees, to lie in a great heep at the bottom of the hole when the skeppe be tooke of it; but we do want the honey, useing a gret lot in the hous for divers things.

Carters wiffe did fall backards and sat in a skeppe of bees, which did make a grett bussing and did send her youping out of the garden; at which Sarah did laff so hartilie, to see Carters wiffe holdeing up her gown while jumping over the cabbiges, that she did neerlie do the same thinge. At which I quite helpless to reprove her, laffing myeself at Carters wiffes spindlie, shankie legs a bobbin up and down among the vegitables. She back anon, with a mighty big nose where a bee had sat up on it, and we to the out hous with the honey skeppes there to leeve them till sure all the bees be gone. Then we shall brake the honey comb up and hit it all upp; and hang it up in a clene cotton bag to run it through; then we shall strain it divers times, and when clere put into the potts reddie to use. Then we shall make honey wine with the comb waxe; to 3 skeppes of wax we do put 2 big messures of water and boil all well till the wax do swim on the top.

This we do skim off and set aside; then we do put the liquor in a vat and while hot do put in it 6 lemons cut in pieces, 6 oringes, like wise 3 pieces of cinamon; then cover all with a clene cloth, and leave 3 days; then we do stur harde for 10 minets by the clock, and leave 3 days; and so on, till 12 days be past. Then strain verrie care-fully in to the cask and to each large messure [? 1 gallon] put 1 quart of best brandie and 3 dried clover blossoms and 1 egg shell broke in fine powder. Leave the bung out of the cask till the clover blows do work out on top of the cask, then bung down verrie tight, and keep a-while before tappeing. The wax we do boil many times till it be a nice yeller culler and no bits of black in it, when it can be stored to use for the pollishing and harness clening.

I can rite no more in my book today; John bein in the house, I fere he may see me.

Oct. ye 2. – Cousin Emmas lad here early with the news that Johns father be ill of a fit, and for John to go at once; so I to the packen of sum clothes not knowing how long he will be away, and he off after a lot of fusse and bother, riding Dobbin, so me left to see to all things.

☙ 13 ☙

ALARUMS FOR ANNE WHILE JOHN IS AWAY

☙

I be verrie sorry for John's mother, she be a dear soul and verrie kind to me when my deer mother died; that I love her much. Later me to the yards to set all going and to tell Carters wiffe to cum and slepe on the kitchen settel to gard us, she bein mighty brave and feering nought. Shepherd in later to say a sheep be cart and ded, and what shall he do with boddie? I tell him to take off the skin and do as he pleases with the rest; and I dout not he will have a feast as never was. But, la, he be welcum, not taisteing meet for many months.

The news spreading that John be gon, cums Mistress Prue to hear all about it. I do tell her all I do know, which be not much, but I do hope Emmas lad will cum soon and we know more.

UNWELCOME VISITOR

Mistress Prue do say are we safe for the night, and I tell her of Carters wiffe cumming, at which she be pleased, and we out to the yards to the milking; and she helping as John be away.

Then seeing Tim safe to the pigg feeding, and to bring the eggs in, we back to find Sarah reddie with the tray; to which we do set to. Sarah eating with us as she do always now, and verrie nice mannered she be, never makeing a noise or putting the bones in her mouth, as so many do: me telling her different. Mistress Prue do tell us that Jane Clarke and Ruth Car did hav a row and Jane did souse a pail of water over Ruth, and did pull her hair, and that Ruth did rip Janes gown to bits; at which Jane wroth and she did smack Ruths face hard as ever she could. At which they do have a gret set to, but they be but drabs and for ever in trubble. Their man did souse water with a pail over them to make them stop it; but they still wrothe and speeke not. Mistress Prue did praise Johns work at Guns Cott much, sayeing it will be verrie good when done. And Carters wiffe cumming in, Sarah and me to walk sum way with Mistress Prue, and in to drink a glass of parsnip wine and home. But we did go to the garden first to see all safe, then supper and to bed, albeit I sumwhat jumpy.

Oct. ye 3. – I did hav a grate frite in the night. Awakeing suddenly, I did hear a queer noise down stairs, and did set up in my bed to harken. It getting louder I did creep to Sarahs room bein verrie frightened, for the noise still goeing on. She roused, we to the top of the stairs to hark once more, then Sarah says me to stop here while she goes to see what ado: but I say no, so we down in to the passidge; Sarah holding the taper, and to the kitchen, where we did rous Carters wiffe, who did now also hear the noise. Then she saying it be cumming from the larder, and tells us to stand by; she off with the grett iron poker to see whats ado, we with her.

She did throw the door open quick and we did see the winder open and a man stuck therin, he not able to go one way or tother. At which Sarah holdeing the taper aloft

Carters wiffe did belabour him with the poker rite valliently about his shulders, and he cursing and trying hard to get away, but he bein tite stuck he could not. Then the Carters wiffe do cry out it be Tim Prew, and I venturing near did see it was, so I did aske him why he did do this, and he did say let him out and he will tell all about it. So Carters wiffe away out side to pull at his legs wile me and Sarah do push him hard. He do go off the winder with a gret bump on his chin which did make him youp.

I fere me Carters wiffe did help it on with a will. Then she holding him in the kitchen and me got over my frite by now, did speke sharp at him to say why he so foolish. And he did say that he bein in the Crowne earlier did make a bet with Carters lad to get in the hous and take out sum vittals.

'DIDD THRESH HIM SOUNDLIE'

At this Carters wiffe do say never her boy do so, but he sayeing if she dont believe, to go quiet to the out hous, and she will see her ladd. She out to see, after giveing Sarah the bigg poker and sayeing to hit him on the hed if he do move, and Sarah promising: she off and we do wait, when she back with her ladd, which do make me so angrie that I did belabur him soundlie with Johns bigg stick. There on he didd start to bellock like a stucke pigge, and his mother didd also thresh him soundlie too, and by the time we end he onlie too glad to get off home. Then didd she serve Tim Prew the same, until he out at last. And I much dout if he will set down cumfurtabel for a while. Then I to put up the bar at the door; when Carters wiffe seeing Tim shaik his fist at us out side the winder, she out after him, whipping his leggs soundlie, giveing him sum rite good smacks; he yoppeting and jumpeing to get away.

Then she back and we to the larder to see the dammidge

done, and do find the latch broken off; and Carters wiffe getting it off the ground didd mend it with a mellett.

CARTER'S WIFE IN DISTRESS

Then we to the kitchen where she do start to cry, sayeing she dont know why her ladd do such things and be so wicked, and she verrie troubled. I do feel verrie sorrie fur her knoweing well it be not her wish or her mans for him to be so. Then Sarah sayeing she will not go to bed again do boil the kettel; and after a cup of tee, bein 4 of the clock we didd dress ourselves, and as soon as light me out to the yard fereing sum mischef done; but all safe so back to the hous to hav a reste, till milking time, letting Carters wiffe and Sarah get the brekfast reddie.

Then all to divers jobs, till cum dinner time when Carters wiffe home with the ham bon and sum oddses to her baskit, and sayeing she will be back before dark.

We bein alone do make a good fire, and did rest, feeling verrie tired. Then Sarah sayeing me to stop in the hous and she will do all in the yards, she to the milkeing, while I do boile the kettel genst her cumming in.

JOHN'S FATHER IS BETTER

Later cums Emmas lad with the nèws that John's father better but do not speke and all use gone from his boddie, which do grief me much. He didd say John will be back cum the middel of the week, and I be verrie glad to know this.

Later cums Farmer Bliss to know if there be ought he can do, so we to the yards where he says all be quite safe. Then he in for a glass of wine sayen he will look at the shepe on his way home. He off after sayeing he will cum agen next day, till John be back home.

It be verrie good of him to do so and I feeleing much safer for it. Then we to bed after barring the doors and the shutters up and Carters wiffe did put Johns blunderbuss to her hand reddie if any boddie try to get in.

But I think me they be verrie glad to keep away, she having a good strong arm and knoweing how to use it.

14

ANNE FALLS ILL AND JOHN'S MOTHER IS
INVITED TO PAY A VISIT

Oct. ye 6. – John did cum home yesternight and we verrie glad to see him. His father be sumwhat better, but do not speak, albeit verrie glad to see him and did know who he was. John verrie angry when I do tell him of Tim Prew and Carters ladds vagaries, but I did tell him how carters wiffe did punnish them both, and to let it pass, there being no harm done. He did praise her much.

Me having a bad pain in my head, I do not rite much in my book, I fear me I did get a cold wile standing in my cold larder in my nite raile, and pushing Tim Prew out.

Nov. ye 2. – It be many days since I did rite in my book, bein ill of a fever, and John fearing much that I should die did worry much; but I nearly well agen and wanting much to go out and look at the pigges and cows. But it be verrie wet and cold, so I must waite a wile. Sarah hav bin a dear good maid nursing me nite and day till John did make her go to her bed to get sum sleep.

Passon Cross be cum to the passonage, bringing his mother to housekeep for him. Sarah tells me she be verrie nice and all do like her much.

Mistress Prue be stopping here till I be well able to go out; she hav bin a great help, and a good friend to us all. She be a dear soul and I do much hope I can be as good a one when I be as old as she, and I pray God I may.

I did fear much for my little booke, when I first ill; and Sarah knowing this did lock it up in the chest and keep the key hid, till I able to hav it.

86

Nov. ye 4. – I down stayers at last, albeit verrie weak, but I be so glad to be in my kitchen once more, and it be all verrie clene and tidie with no grease spots on the floor as I feared. Today John did tell me that his father did die, cum two weeks agoe, but I so ill he said nought, and did stay home; his mother saying he to stop with me, and never mind her, she doing best she could.

It do greave me much that she should have this trubble, and I did beg John to go to her now, me bein much better, and Mistress Prue and Sarah doing all for me I do do verrie well. At this John do say he will go cum the morn, and will ask Farmer Ellis to look to the working of the farm, at which I verrie glad, for I do know well his dear mother must need him. So he starting at 6 of the clock.

Nov. ye 5. – John off to his Mother this morn after the same fuss and bother he do always make when going on a journie; while I in bed till 10 of the clock, Mistress Prue saying it be best for me after such a bad time, and indeed I do coffe much. I did bid Sarah to lite a fire in the best parlour so we could sit there after all the work be done. And later cums Mistress Cross, passons mother, to see how I do. She be a verrie plessent boddy and much like her son, who she do seem to love verrie much. She saying how hard he did work when his father died to get on and give her a good home: which he have done. I did say was all cumfurtabel, me having to leave all to Mistress Prue, and she did say all was verrie nice, and me to go when well enuff and see for myself. She did thank me for being good to her son when he first cum; then she home, after drinking a cup of my Chiny tee, with a baskit of butter and eggs and a bottel of my primmy rose wine, the which she had never heard of before.

Sarah did pack it up for her.

Farmer Ellis in later to say all is well, and we begging him to stop a while he did so, and Sarah did bring him Johns pipe and bacca, as well as a jug of best cider; and we all verrie snug in the best parlour, and after he gone we to bed. I do wish John was back for I do miss him much. Mistress Prue do share my bed chamber for fear I do need ought in the nite. I do fear they will kill me with kindness, they be all so good to me.

JOHN MEETS A FOOTPAD

Nov. ye 7. – Carters wiffe here early for the washing of cloes, and Mistress Prue to the butter making.

Later the sun shining out bravely, Mistress Livvie did get out the cart and Nancy, and after cuvvering me up well, did take me a outing; which was verrie plessent after being in the hous so long. We did meet divers folks who did all say they glad to see me better, and Passon did cum to the cart to talk, then we back, the sun bein gone.

Sarah getting the tee reddie, we sat to the tabel, and I saying how much better I did feel for the outing they all verrie pleased, and did much fun.

Later cums Carters Wiffe in to say the spottie sowe be making of her bed, and she had better sit with her reddie for the little pigges cumming, to which I agree, not wanting to loos any with John away. But I did tell her to sit in the warm kitchen and go out whiles, and Sarah did put a jug of cider on the hob to warm for her to drink, it being cold of nites now. Then me to rite in my book.

I be much better today my ride did do me good, and I do feel that God be verrie good to me and I be grateful to his mercy for giving me so many kind friends, yet I do feel I have done nought to deserve it.

*

Nov. ye 10. – John safe this morn having rode the brown mare all nite. I do thank God he be home safe, for he did tell us that half way home a man did say he wanted money and would have it. At which John did tell him he would get nought from him, then the man did say suddenly, was he ought to do with Master Hughes up along Raymeddowe?

John was verrie struck at this he not knowing the man at all. Then the man did say Johns voice did sound like Thomas Hughes and he did have a look of him. Whereon John did say it was his father who was but just now dead, then the man did say he verrie vexed he had stopt him, or thought to rob him, for his father and mother had saved him from jail when all agen him, and he would do nought but good for Master Hughes and his family, and did ask John pardon; where-on John did give him a ginney and bad him go his gait which he did, and John home safe.

JOHN INVITES HIS MOTHER

He do say that his mother not liking to live at the farm now her good man be gone, he did counsel her to sell all and cum with us till a hous be found for her. Whereon I do say why bother about a hous? – but to cum and live with us, for we all love her and I would be so glad of it and could make her feel at home, me telling Sarah she verrie pleased and did say she would do all she could to make her happy. And so John be sending Tim with a letter to his mother to cum here, and I do long for the time to cum to have her with us. She bein a dear sweet boddy.

John did praise carters wiffe hugely for her care of the spottie sowe, there bein 12 good piggies and all strong. John did tell her she shall have one for her stye when it be old enouf, which pleased her mightily. And he did thank Mistress Prue and her sister for their care of me, and did send old Joe to Ivy Cottage with a fletche of our best bakon to repay their kindness; he so pleased I be better, bless him.

꿍 15 꿍

A WELCOME FOR MISTRESS HUGHES

꿍

Nov. ye 14. – I have not written in my book for some days being busy getting the house clene from garret to cellar in readinesse of Johns mother cumming. Sarah be mitie pleased and do work with a will, saying she will do anything for such a dear lady. Later John cums in to say Farmer Bliss have had two cowes die of a fever and that he feares more will die, at which John do not go near; fearing for our own cowes, which we should be sorrie to lose. Then John to the milking and we to divers jobbes till John in to supper; and for Sarah to cook him a dish of ham and egges, he bidding me to rest for I be verrie tired from so much scrubbing. So to bed earlie after seeing all safe for the nite.

JOHN HAS A BIRTHDAY

Nov. ye 18. – This be Johns birthday. I did give him a pair of blue velvit britches which my dear lady's mother did give me in my parsell, and which pleased him mitilie, he liking good small cloes to his leg cuvvering.

Sarah did give him a fine white handkercher with his name broydered on it by herself, which he liked verrie much and did thank her rite hartilie; and later Mistress Prue did send a boy with a bottle of her eldern berrie wine for us to drink his health and long life, which me and Sarah did with much pleasure, for her be verrie kind to us.

90

Then me to the roasting of a green goose for dinner, and a great big appel pie and a egge custard, and did warm sum furzzie wine with ginger, agen John cumming in; which he did enjoy, it bein a verrie cold and stormy day.

He did say the dinner the best he ever tasted, he liking the stuffing which I made like this:

2 big hand fulls of stale bred crums, a onion chopt, 2 rosie appels chopt up, a cup of sweet plums [raisins?], 4 hard boiled egges chopt verrie small, a pinch of pepper and a pinch of dark sugger, and sum fat bakon. This be all chopt up together and mixed with enuff cream to make it all stick together, then put in the goose before roasting. It be verrie sweet eating.

PARTY PREPARATIONS

Nov. ye 27. — I have had such a mint of work to do, I have had no time to rite in my book till now. John's mother did cum 2 days agon, and rite glad I be to have her, bless her. She did say she would leave us later, thinking we would like best to be by our selfes in our home: but we say not so and that we do all want her, and so it be settled, to our great content. She did work verrie hard for John to make him the good man he is, so now it be our turn to show what we can do to repay her good work, and she do be verrie worthy of it all. Day after to-morrow we be having a little partie, albeit quiet, so now I back down stairs to Sarah, after putting my little book away safe.

CARTER'S WIFE TO HELP

Dec. ye 1. — We did have a verrie good time yester-eve, we having Farmer and Mistress Bliss, Farmer and Mistress Jones, Passon and his mother and Mistress Prue and her sister. Carters wife did cum in to help with the cooking earlie, so we did get all reddie, and I did bring out my glass and silver which did look verrie fine and made a goodlie show.

STUFFED SLICES OF HAM

We did do much cooking, and Johns mother did show us how to do ham a new way. She did cut sum slices out of the middle of the big ham, and did spread them with chopt herbs and sweet plums, and then roll them up and tie verrie tight, and boil softly for 30 minutes of the clock; then place out on a dish to get cold. This did look verrie dainty when piled up cross ways on a fine glass dish. We did also have a rump of sheep mutton roasted, and a piece of beef boiled, and 3 hens and a goose roasted, appel pies and tarts and custard puddens, and divers others and butter and cheese and bredde; and to drink they did have sum beer and cider, and a bottel of brandy, and sum of my primy rose wine which be 4 years old and good drinking.

MISTRESS PRUE DID PLAY

Johns mother did bring from her own chest sum silver candel stickes, each of them taking three tapers, which did look mightly fine down the middle of the table.

We did not dance out of respect to John's father, but the men did talk and smoke their pipes, and we ladies did talk also; and Mistress Prue did play sum verrie prettie bits on my spinette, with both hands, much to our delight.

Later Johns mother do find that she and Passons mother did know each other, they bein near naybours in their girl hood days; but not meeting since. This did delight me much, for now Johns mother will hav her old friend near to talk to. Sarah did cum to sitt with us, and Passons mother was much taken with her moddist ways which Johns mother did say was all my training. I fear me much that Passon be falling in love with her, and I doute not I shall lose her later on. He did cum and sitt with us and I did see him looking at Sarah much.

Later when all gone, we to bed, after all fastened up safe for the nite. Mistress Jones did say Mary be doing verrie well, and have got a good man, but I doute if he be as good as my John.

WHO DID THIS MISCHIEF?

Dec. ye 4. – John in from the yard verrie vexed at the cowes all gone astray; sum body opening the shed doors and letting them loose they be all gone, and John thinks it be Carters ladd and Tim Prew, and do say he will horse whip them soundlie when he do catch them. I was much vexed at having no milk to use, and at the loss of the creme therto.

Then John off, taking carter and Tim to look for the cowes; and Johns mother did wunder if they be stole, as such things do happen sum wiles, and ours be verrie good beasties.

We to the house work albeit I verrie trubbled, not knowing what to think.

❧ 16 ❧

CARTER'S LAD IN MISCHIEF AGAIN

❧

Later cums Farmer Bliss to say he had heard the cowes be gon and to say his Carter do say that he did see sum on the road past his cott early this morn with 2 men driving them. At this I do ride off on Nancy to see for myself, and meeting John I do tell him; so we off but do find no trace, so me back home not liking to look at the empty stalls.

Johns mother be reddie with the dinner, but we no heart

to the eating of it. Then says Sarah had master thought to go the lower lane way, and I say I think not; so Johns mother riding Dobbin and me Nancy, off we go to the lower lane, a dirtie feckless road, no body do ever use; and there we do see our cowes in a paddock.

THE COWES ARE FOUND

Then, says Johns mother, we must take them back; so we do fetch them out and we do drive them home, and into the sheds; much to our delight. And poor things they glad too, but sum body had had the morns milk from their gags, so we did leave them till cum milking time.

John in later we do tell him all, and he did give Sarah a silver piece and say she be the clever one to give us the hint, he bein verrie glad. Then says John he will find out who did play such a trick on us, and we to say nought about it. I fear I have lost much butter through it which is not good for my pocket.

A REVENGEFUL TRICK

John in to tea do say he will go to the Crown, and perhaps find out who did take the cowes astray. So me and Sarah putting all reddie for the nite, he off anon, and we to our nitting of stockings. Then he back agen, and saying by the talk he do hear, that it be Carters ladd and Tim Prew who do it, and they do laff much at our to do.

John be verrie angry and do say he shall tell Carter cum morn to get off and he will have another man to work. But I like not his doing this, and do say the father and mother are to be pitied not blamed, and Johns mother do say this too, and that she verrie sorry for them; and if she were John she would whipp them both verrie soundlie, but not to punnish the parents who can help nought.

94

John then saying he will not turn Carter away, we both glad and I do fetch him a mug of my dandie lion wine at which he do call me a baggage, and his mother as well; and we do all laff, but I be so glad carter and his wife will not suffer for their sons misdeeds.

Dec. ye 7. – Carters wiffe here to help us with the cleaning of the dairy and passidges, she be verrie trubbled for her ladds misdeeds, whereby she do dry her tears and to work. I later to the yards with Sarah, whereon she do cry out carters ladd be there and me to cum quick she holding him, so I with a great stick do belabour him soundlie for his trick with the cowes. Whereon he do say he will do so agen. I so wroth at this I do box his ears many times so hard as I can, that he soon begging for mercy, and letting him be off, with Sarah after him with a whip, getting in sum good wacks to his legs, much to his discumfort.

SARAH GETS HER OWN BACK

I fear me she did but settle an old score; then she back and to the milking and we bussie, and anon back to the house, and Sarah telling Johns mother of the beating, they do laff hartily, and John cumming in do ask whats ado. And Sarah tells him at which he sorry it be not he who was there and he out to tell carter to keep him away, he not having him on the ground agen. I fear he is a bad ladd, and I be sorrie for the parents who be hard working and honest as the day.

Later we do much nitting of hose by the fire. We did have sum snow and it be verrie cold.

I be glad the cowes and pigs have got warm sheds to sleep in this weather, and not have to lie in the cold.

Dec. ye 13. – Cums today a message from the Passonage for me and Johns mother to go tea drinking and to take Sarah if we so mind. So Johns mother to carters wiffe to tell her to cum and look to Johns tea and the pigge feeding, and then we bussie to leave all tidie agenst our goeing out.

Sarah was verrie pleased and did say what gown should she wear to do me credit, so we up to my chamber where I did give her a purple velvitt out of my chest, and did give it her to put on. It fitted her finely, so I did tell her to wear it with her warm cloke and nitted bonnitt.

I did wear my red velvitt with the black lace kerchef and Johns mother did put on her black velvitt with the white flowere and fur cloke and bonnitt, then we off. John bowing us out the door saying he verrie honnered to live with such fine ladies. It was verrie cold, but we soon warm agen by a good fire. Passons mother did give us a good welcome and did talk to Sarah verrie kind, and she soon talking to Johns mother of old times. I to asking how Passon liked living here, to which he says he and his mother verrie happy and cumfortable, and he will not forget our kindness that first Sabbath; for he was verrie nervous, it being the first sermon he did ever give; to which I did tell him he did verrie well. His mother did question me much about Sarah, saying she be a pretty wench and nice mannered. I did agree saying she as good as she is pretty, we trusting her always, to which Johns mother do agree also. Then we home agen to find carters wife with some hot toddie reddie for us. It did start to snow later.

MERRYMAKING IN THE HUGHES HOUSEHOLD

❧

Dec. ye 15. – It have snowed so hard this 2 days, that we be quite cut off from every body by the deep drifts. John and sheperd did have to dig the sheep out which was burried under the snow and make a road for them to walk home to the yards. It do look verrie strange from the winders to see nought but snow, it be verrie cold and the house verrie dark with so much snow agen the walls. I be thankful there be plentie to eat. I do pray there be no dum things cast away in the snow. Carter and shepherd did have to dig their way to work, and Johns mother and Sarah did dig to the pigges and calfs. The snow do make a bad mess on my clene kitchen floors, but Sarah do clean with a will, so it not too bad. Bein bussie I cannot rite more now.

SNOW BE ALL GONE

Dec. ye 19. – I have had no time for writing in my book for sum days. The snow be all gone, and all the roads be deep in mud, so that we out only on horse back and do put on our patterns to sweep the yard place.

Carters ladd be off for a soldier and a verrie good thing too for he will be safe and not trubble his mother any more. Tim Prew be gone also, it were he who did make carters ladd wild.

Farmer Jones did lose many sheep in the snow, and sum pigges have bin drowned in the flood water. I be glad ours are all safe. John do say we on the hill the water do run away from us. It be but 6 days to Christmas, and I do hope the mud will be all gone by then, for Johns cusson Tom be cumming, and Emma and her ladd and his sweetheart. We have not heard how Mistress Prue and her sister have fared in the snow but passon did cum up on his grey cob to see how we do, and I verrilie believe it was mostly to see Sarah; but he did not, she being at the bed making.

Later cums John all muddy and water dripping from his britches seat; he slipping up and sat in a great puddel when feeding the pigges. He verrie wroth and did romp about my clene kitchen floor which did vex me sore, but me knowing his temper did go warilie; so up to fetch his dry clothes, the while he out to the pump to wash the mud from his face and out of his hair. He better after a hot drink, out agen, me not daring to laff till he gone, albeit we fit to bust our selfes at John all muddy.

Yet I did laff too soon for me and Sarah out to the pump for a pail of water, down I did go a proper bump in the mud; me catching at Sarah she down atop of me and the pail falling on her head; and thereat, Johns mother out to see what all the cabbel be about, did laff much at me lying in the mud with Sarah atop, crowned with the pail.

A GOOD MEAT CAKE

Sarah laffing much I do beg her to get off me to let me rise, so she up, still laffing and me up, a sorrie spectacle too, with the muddy water dripping from my gown, and I did hurry in to get rid of it lest John should see and laff last after all.

We soon clean and tidy, and after we to the hemming of sheets, and John did mend sum harness and divers things, then supper and to bed.

Dec. ye 23. – We have bin verrie bussie with sum goodlie things to eat. Boiled hams and great big mince pies and roast geese and hens and boiled and roasted beef, all reddie for eating. Johns mother be going to make a pudden for carter and shepherd, and I shall give them a big mince pie and apples, so that they can have Christmas fare. Carters wiffe be cumming early to get ready for our visitors who be cumming tomorrow. We shall be verrie bussie, so I shall not have time to write in my book till all over.

Johns mother have made a verrie pretty dish wich she do call meat cake. She did mix flower and butter to a thick paste and put sum on the bottom of a bake tin, this she did cover with the chopt beef and onion and herbs, then more paste, then more meat and flavouring, and paste agen, till the tin be full. Then she do cover all with more paste and cook till done. She do say this do cut like a cake when it be cold with the meat inside. There be also 2 roast hares and pudden with spices and plenty of apple pies and divers things and junkets, cider cake and cinnamon cakes and a rich Christmas cake, Johns mother did bake.

I hope we shall have enough, but I be keeping sum rabbit pies and a big ham ready, in case it be wanted. John will tap the new beer and the honey wine, and we shall have primy rose wine, as well as Eldernberrie, and dandie lyon, so there should be good store.

I do hear John below so must not write more; I do love my little book so do write much and have wrote nearly all the pages, and I dout if I shall start another one, though I do love it.

JOURNEY BY PACK HORSE

Dec. ye 27. – Christmas be all over now, and our visitors gone, but a right good time we did have, the roads did dry up a bit so not too bad for the travellers, who did cum pack horse. Cusson Tom and Emma, her ladd and his sweetheart Jan, did get here after a journie of hard going Christmas Eve, the rest did cum Christmas morning and all of us to church leaving carters wiffe and Sarahs sister Jane to help Sarah with the dinner to be all ready genst our cumming back, and mother and me did set the tables together in a row and cover them with my linnen table cloths; then we did put the silver and glass and all did look verrie fine. Passon did give a verrie good sermon, telling us to do to others as we would have them do to us, and the world the better place, to which I do agree. The singing did go right heartilie with a great roar, the church bein full, for all do like the young passon and his mother.

WE DID STEP IT OUT

Then we out and home to our dinner. John did set at one end with the beef and geese, and Farmer Ellis at the other to cut up the hams and so on, which Sarah and Jane did carry round till all served, and all did eat their fill and had plentie. Then John did pass the wine and all did drink each other's healths; then the men did smoke while we ladies did drink our wine and talk of divers things that had happened through the year, not thinking so much had; then the men did say let us dance, so Bill and Jen did play a merrie jig on their fiddles and we did step it out finely; till all breathless, we do sit down laffing much.

THE GAME OF POPP

Farmer Bliss did say lets have a story, so Passon did tell us a good one that did cause much merriment; then John did say he would tell them the story what happened when his father died, and did tell of the man what stopped him on the road. His mother did say it must have bin Joe Graves who did go to them for shelter when in trouble, and they did hide him for 3 days and he getting off safe at last. Then said Mistress Prue it showed how one good turn did make another.

Then cusson Tom saying we be getting too serious, so

Mistress Prue to the spinette to play a merrie tune, and we to dancing once more stepping it right merrilie till Sarah do say its time for tea; whereon we do sit down and do justice to all the good things provided, which did make a brave show and looked verrie good on the dishes; the lights from the tapers in Johns mothers silver candle sticks did light the holly Sarah had put on the table in glasses. All the ladies did like mothers meat cake, and want to know how to make it.

Then we did gather together and play the game of Popp; we did put the chairs in a ringe, the men on one side, the ladies on the other with our hands behind, one holding a apple which be passed from one to another. The man must not speak but do beckon to the lady they think have got the apple; if she have not she do say 'popp' and the man do have to sit on the floor and pay forfitt, till all there; but if he be right he do take the ladie on his knees till the game be played out. After we did play bobbie apple, and snap draggon, the Passon burning his fingers mitilie to get Sarahs plum; all did enjoy it much, and then we did stop a while for sum cakes and wine, and sum songs sung by one and other; then more dancing till supper, then more games and later all home after a really good Christmas which we did all enjoy much with everybody happie. And now this be the last page in my little book. I know not if I shall ever write another one. I do feel I have much to be thankful for, for my life with John and his mother be a verrie happy one.

I do wonder where my little book will go, who may read it. I shall always keep it, and perhaps if God do give me a son he will read it some day and so know what a fine man his father is. So I say good-by to my little book.

[*But Anne does not say good-bye to her Journal for long. In the next chapter you will read of the new book given to her — and how she proceeds to fill it.*]

A DISH FOR CROSS HUSBANDS

ల

[Anne Hughes starts a new year with a new book for her Journal.]

Jan. ye 3. – John's mother did laff verrie much at me, finding out I did write our doings in a little book, and did also give me this one to write more of our doings as they do come to pass. The weather be most cold, and the frost did freeze the new milk in the pannes this morn, thus spoiling it for the butter making; much to my distress, for I like not to see so much waste. John cumming in do say that the black sow have killed all her little pigges, and he so wroth thereby he do forget to drink his hot toddie, and did tell Sarah to come out to the yards, and we to stop our caddel in the kitchen. At this me verrie cross, but he being off I did saye nought, but did get on to the cooking.

A HEAVY SNOWFALL

Later cums Passon Cross to talk to John, and it being near supper time, me and Sarah to the spinning of yarne and Johns mother to the nitting of hose, gainst the time they be needed. Then, Passon gone, we to bed.

I fear that he will take Sarah from us later. I did see his talk was but a faddel to get to see her, and I like it not, for she be a good wench and verrie useful to me.

Jan. ye 4. – This morn we did wake up to see every place covered with snow, it falling right heartilie in the night, and work on the land be at the stand still; nought bein done but

to feed the stock. So today we plagued mightilie with John in the house, bringin this and that to do and mend, till my clean kitchen be verrie sluty with the snow he do bring in; and me so wroth there at, I do say to get out to the back-house with his messy jobbes, and so he goes off there-to, saying never was a man so plagued with a parcel of women, they being the verrie divvel round a man. At which we laffing, he do stamp out, banging the door mightilie.

Later me to the making of an apple pudding genst his coming in agen, and Sarah did take him out a good jorum of hot punch, whereby he better tempered on return. I do so mislike snow, it be so verrie messie, and do make a great lot of work to keep the floors clean.

Jan. ye 7. – Passon cums in to say he will not hold service with such winter weather, and deep snow; he having hard work to dig his way here. We very glad to see him, so he to dinner with us and eating hearty of the stuffed ham and apple pie John's mother had cooked.

JOHN'S VIOLET PUDDING

He did say that Mistress Prue was sick of a cold but on the mend agen; also that Farmer Bliss had lost a calf of the black scour, at which John's Mother did say he should make and drench them with a drink made of some crushed pepper cornes and ginger, mixed with some pudding flour and gin; this bein the best cure of all, whereby she had cured many of her own. Then Passon off with a basket of my eggs and sum butter for his Mother, who be a verrie nice body, we do all like. Then we to bed after seeing all is safe, John saying it be warmer out and the snow melting, for which I be thankful after shivering in my bed nights of late.

Jan. ye 9. – Carters wiffe cum this morn; the snow be mostly gone now, but the mud be verrie deep, it being up to our knees in parts. We to the washing of clothes and the baking of bread and such like for the week's eating. John in later to put on dry small clothes, he sitting in a mud puddle with his back seat and verrie wroth thereby, and later he to market with some old ewes which be no more use.

Later his Mother do make a violet pudding for when he do cum back from market, it being a good cure for cross husbands. This is how it be made: You take of the dried blossoms 6 handfuls and boil gently till verrie tender, then chop verrie fine; next mix with 6 eggs whipt to a froth with a big spoonful of bee honey and the juice of a lemon.

Put in a greased dish and bake till set, then drop some of the dried violets verrie fine and sprinkle atop, and eat it with plenty of cream. This be verrie good for giddyness of the head and verrie light and toothsome. I did also make him a Jinnie Jones as well.

It be made this way: Chop up a big sliver of boiled ham with 3 eggs boiled verrie hard, a cup of bread crumbs, pepper and salt, some sage and onion, all chopped verrie fine. Then mix all verrie well together with three egges beaten to a froth, so that all do stick together, then put to bake to 20 minutes of the clock. This be verrie good when eaten with potatoes baked in the oven in their skins, and eaten with plenty of butter.

John back anon verrie pleased at the price he did get for the old ewes, they making three shillen apiece. When fed he do say he did meet Master Peters, his Mother's old naybour, he did say he would much like to see her; and John liking much to give his mother pleasure did tell him he be welcome to come. She also very pleased, and he cumming on Saturday.

UNTIMELY PROPOSAL

Jan. ye 12. – Being bussie I have not writ in my book for sum two days. Master be cum and it did make much cooking and cleaning, it bein so muddy every way, and I liking my house to be sweet and clean.

Carters wiffe be here to help Sarah with the work, John misliking he Mother or me to do the dirtie part. Master Peters be a nice man, verrie hearty with his feelings, and I do like him verrie well.

Jan. ye 15. – Master Peters did go home today, and thereby hangs a tale; for it do seem he did but come for the purpose of asking John's Mother to wed him, and he getting her to his selfe in the back yarde did pop the question. At which she did let out at him finely, and threatened to belabour him with the yarde besom, saying he should be ashamed, and her own dear man but lately buried. Where by she did take him by the neck and did shake him till he did yowl for mercie, and me going out did rescue him, and later he off.

✌ 19 ✌

THE GUESTS ARRIVE FOR ANNE'S PARTY

✌

Jan. ye 24. – Today we all mightie bussie with the cooking reddie for tomorrow's partie. John's mother did showe me how to make a new pudden to eat colde, and we taisting a piece did find it verrie good.

This is how it be made: Take 6 apples with the pipps out and leaving on the skin, cut in verrie thin slivers and lay in the bottum of a dish. Cover well with black sugar, and sum fat [suet?] chopt verrie small. Cover all with bred crumbs well soaked with brandy, then more apple slivers and chopt fat, and sugar, then more crumbs well soaked with the brandy; then break 3 egges in a bowl and beat up with a spoon till frothie, with a measure of the brandy, and pour over all, then cook in the bake oven for 30 minutes by the clock. When it is verrie cold, take a measure of cream and beat it up till it be verrie stiff, but not butterie, and put over the toppe in lumps.

This be a verrie daintie dish and good eating.

Then we did stuff a great ham, and Mistress Prue cummen in for her butter do showe us how to make a new drink this way: She did take a bottle of my primmy rose wine and put in a jugge, then 2 egges, 2 spoonfuls of bee honnie, a measure of brandy, and 2 lemons cut up. She did not use the yaller egge parte, taking only the white, and, covering all, did let stand for 2 hours. Then with my bigge silver spoon she did beat all together till white and verrie frothie. Then covering again for 10 minutes she did strain all through a muslin cloth and bottle. There bein sum over John was called in to taist. He do saye it hath a verrie pretty flavour. What is it? And Mistress Prue laffinge do say juste his own wine in a newe gowne; and he bein pleased did say, we would call it newe gowne wine and pussel all who drink it.

GOOD HONNIE PIE

We did also make divers pies and little cakes, and also a honnie pie which John's mother did make. It be verrie nice and simple to make: put plentie of fat on the sides and bottum of a dish, then put in a good layer of crumbs, and cover verrie thick with honnie and sweet plums, then more crums, and cover all with 4 egges beaten up with a little measure of cream. Then put on sweet plums in divers ways all over the toppe and cook in the oven for ten minutes of the clock.

There be a goodlie show now to our larder shelffes.

Jan. ye 26. – John being out to Passon Crosses, I can write in my little book in cumfurt.

Our partie did go verrie well, we having the fiddelers here to make sweet musick. Carters wiffe and Sarah's sister Jane did cum to help, John sayeing Sarah must join us.

Mistress Prue and her sister did cum earlie to help lay the table, with my best dammy [damask?] cloth and they did fill little pottes with box and hollie, and put on the table, Mistress Prue saying all the qualitie do do so; so I verrie pleased thereby.

Later we up stairs to put on our gownes readie for the partie. John's mother did make a verrie pretty figger in her black velvit gown with sum fine lace at her throat and elbows. She be such a daintie little boddie and I do so love to look at her when she be sitting in her bigge chair, she be so pleasant to look at, she be so sweet a boddie.

I did wear my spottie silk, and shoes with the silver buckles. Passon and his mother did cum furst of them all, and later Master and Mistress Bliss, and anon Farmer and Mistress Ferris from Lower Layes; then we all readie and to the best kitchen to eat. Everybodie bein clem of their walking did eat in fine style, and did do justis to the good things. All did like mother's pudden, and Mistress Cross did ask howe it be done, she liking much the lumpie cream on toppe.

GAME OF NIDDIE NODDIE

Then all bein full up, I did hand round the wine for the ladies, and the men having their wine and pipes, we to the best parlour to gossip, talking of divers things.

Mistress Ferris did say that her sister did die cum three months agon, and did leave her all to divers folk, not thinking of her at all; but, says she, what mattered it, she bein of a warm pockett, she needed nought. Then says Mistress Bliss it be not the ones that do brag that do have the most monies to shake.

So me seeing they did not agree did change the talke sum

what by saying for them to try our newe drinke. And Sarah fetching in the bottles all did drink sum, and ask what it is, it bein such nice drinking.

Then says John's mother, ask Mistress Prue who did make it: and she telling how, they all vow to make sum likewise.

Then the men cumming in, John do say let us dance. So the fiddelers did strike up and we did foot it right heartilie, keepen it up til we be all breathless and glad of a rest. So we did sit down and after the wine had been passed, Farmer Bliss did say what about a game of Niddie Noddie, to play, the whiles we did rest; so we did gather round in a ring on our chairs, and did put John in the middle for the Niddie Noddie. It be a fine game and is played this way.

We do sit in a ring with the Noddie in the middle, then we keeping our hands at our backs, so not to be seen, do pass a thimble verrie quick round to this one and that, both back and forth, and the Noddie do have to nod his head at the one with the thimble. He be wrong more often than not all the time, and looking so funnie. Later all ready to eat agen, we fall to and soon most of the dishes be used up. Sarah and John's mother do bring in a great bowl of steaming hot punch, in which we do all dip our glasses and drink the health of everie boddie.

Mistress Cross did call me aside and say could Sarah drink tee with her cum tomorrow. This pleased me mightilie, and I did say yes; at which she do say she would like that her son would wed her, she having great reggard for her.

Then all saying it be getting late the ladies soon cloaked and bonitted, and off, and John out to the yardes to see all is safe, then he to bed, the while his mother and me do put away my silver spoons and forks in a safe place till next time, and after barring the doors and shutters, we to bed also.

❧ 20 ❧

VANISHMENT OF A BLACK COW

❧

Jan. ye 27. – John in this morn with the newes that the black cowe be gone, he not knowing where; there bein no sign. So he fears she be took away in the night. I be verrie vexed and John verrie wroth, and so he do go to Squire Manton to ask what to do. Then he back, and seeing us all in the back house do say, be we going to caddel all the day with our tungues waggen; which do make me verrie angrie, we bin hard at it sorting the apples; and do say bother his old cowe; and this did make him so mad he did hop about the floor like a pea in a hens croppe, and did kick the apples this way and that in his temper. And his Mother, seeing we both put out, do take him to the kitchen for a hot possit she had made reddie genst his cummen. So he soon better tempered, and off agen to search for the lost cowe, taking carter with him, and for we to do the milking and pigge feeding, and divers jobbes with old Joe.

We into dinner, and later hard at it till dark; and John not back, we do eat by our selves.

It bein dark night I do get verrie fidgetty, thinking John have cum to sum harm, but his mother say not to worrie, he quite able to care for himself. But I was verrie glad to see him cum in later; with no news of the cowe which he fears be gone for good.

A STRANGE BEAST AT MARKET

Jan. ye 29. – It be two days since the cowe was lost, and we do now think she be carried off and sold somewhere, and so we to be the losers. John be verrie grumpie thereat, and yesterday did cloute young Jim finely for braken a egge, and I did give the lad a lump of cake to stop his howling, feeling sorrie for him.

John be verrie unluckie of late, for later the brindel cowe did kick the pail of milk over, at which John did thresh her soundlie. I fear me he will serve us the same likewise if the black cowe be not found. I be verrie sorrie she be gone, for she be a verrie easie milker, and no vice in her.

Feb. ye 1. – To-day cums Master Ellis with the news that he be told of a strange black beast bein seen over to the market and thinks it may be ours. So John up and he off, after a drink of cider, to make sure; and we to the scrubbing of floors and odd jobbes. Johns mother did clean the winders and they do now shine verrie bright, so that we do se verrie clear. I do always like my winders to be clean and bright, for dirty ones do show that the mistress be a sluttie boddie.

Then Sarah and carters wiffe to the yardes to the milking and pigge feeding, and me and John's mother to the cooking of a good supper for John's return. When it be darke, we to the sewing of some new sheets, of which I have nowe a goodlie store, and if Sarah be wed to Passon – as I much fear she will be – I shall give her some to her linen chest.

John in anon with the news that he have got the cowe, but fears she may have a fever, not bein milked this 3 days, so his mother to the making of a drink to cure it. This how it be made. Take of crushed pansie seeds one spoonful, a bigge spoonful of 'ladds love' chopt up verrie fine, 2 egges and a measure of cream, all beaten up together with some hot water to make all warm to the drinking.

TO BUY SOME HEIFERS

John in anon after dosing the cowe, and he do tell us he did meet in with Master Perry of Churchland, who do want to buy some heifer calfs, so he be coming at morn to look to ours, we having some to spare.

Later sending Sarah to bed I do tell John's mother my fears lest Passon should carry off Sarah to wed: and she did say why not, they be both young with life before them, let them be happy; and we would say nought agen it, but help all we can. But said I, I know not how I can do with no Sarah to help me. Then said she, we could manage verrie well with carters wife, and Sarah's sister Jane to come in days. To which I do agree, but I like not the thought of letting Sarah go from me, but I must be ready for it, although I do almost wish that Passon had stopt away.

A GINGERBREAD MAN

Feb. ye 4. – Yesterday we busie with the washen of clothes and the baken of bredd and other oddses, and later me and John's mother to market to take my butter and egges to sell. The roads be verrie muddy, so that we did bump much, and had much trouble to get along with old Dobbin. I do allus like going to the market, it be verrie nice to get in cumpanie sumtimes.

I did sell my butter for 7 pence a pound, and 6 pence a score for the egges which are now dearer, and so brings more monies to my stocken.

I did buy a ribbon for Sarah's hair, and a gingerbred man, as well as one for Carters wiffe, and a packet of bacca for John, as well as divers things we do want. Then we back home, it bein a messie day and verrie cold, so we glad to get back to my warm kitchen, where Sarah had got a nice hot meal ready for our cummen.

I did give her the ribbon and ginger man to her great pleasure, she saying she did love me for so much kindness. And Carters wiffe pleased also. Then John cummen in I did give him his bacca, and he soon sitten in his chair apuffen away at his pipe. Then, after sending Carters wiffe home with sum oddses for her supper, we soon abed, bein tired of our journey.

≈ 21 ≈

DISTURBANCES IN THE LARDER

≈

Feb. ye 6. – This morn we did hear a great shouting cum from the yardes, so out to see what's ago, and did find that the bull had got hold of Joe in his pen, and not letting him out agen, so he skeert.

I not sure what to do, when Sarah did go in to him and the bull knowing her, did cum away; whereat she did ketch up old Joe by the seat of his small clows, and did push him over the manger tother side and outen danger. She be a brave lass, and strong, and we did laffe heartilie at old Joe who did make for his cott afeared the bull were still after him.

Then Sarah to the feeding of the bull, bein now good agen. I fear me old Joe did do sum hurt to him, for he be a verrie quiet beast all ways. Then me back to the house to find Mistress Prue cum to tell us it be much safer to keep all the doors and winders barred, it bein said thieves braken in to folks houses, and that Mary Trimmer had lost sum portaties but yesterday. Thinking that John may have monies in the house, she fears for him much.

This do make me verrie frightened.

NOISE IN THE KITCHEN

Feb. ye 11. – Yesternite we did have a great big fright. We bein tired did go to bed at 6 of the clocke, and soon were

113

asleep, when later cums John's mother in to our bedchamber to say she did hear a noise to the kitchen.

John not being willing to leave his warm bed did say it be nought but the wind ablowing, but she now listening to him did say for him to go and see whats ado. At this John, albeit grumbling much, do put on his small cloes and hose and taken his bigge stick from behind the door; he down, and Sarah also roused, and she saying that she do hear also, we all down, albeit me verrie frightened.

We did see nought in the kitchen, but Sarah going to the larder did cry out for us to go and see; and we in and did see the meat be all gone from the plate, with only sum scrappie bittes left. We all verrie scared at this, and John did look to the winder, and we all amazed to find it be still barred inside, and the bolt in place. Then says John's mother someboddie be here for sure, so we to the searching of the house; but did find nought, every place being the same as when we did go to bed overnite.

So we to bed agen, and John's mother and Sarah did stop in our bedchamber till dawn.

I was verrie pusselled for somebodie did eat the ham, but we know not who or how.

Feb. ye 13. – Cums a man from Mistress Ellis to ask will John go over, Master Ellis bein ill of a fit and not speaking. So he off and we to divers jobbs out and in.

John cums back later to say Master Ellis be verrie restless and that he will go back and stoppe the night there. So I did send Sarah for Carter's wife to cum and sleep in the kitchen on the settel for our protection; she have a good arm for hitting and we be still verrie pusselled over the loss of the ham, not hearing anything queer through the day.

John gone, we did bar all the doors and windows and made sure all was safe. Then said Sarah let us stop in the kitchen with Carter's wiffe for companie. At which me verrie glad, not liking the thought of sleeping in my bedchamber with John out of the house. Then Sarah did bring the two bigge chairs from the best parlour, and sum pillows for me and John's mother, and so we verrie comfortable round a good fire, and later we did start to dose asleep.

THE LOGS WERE STOLEN

Later Sarah did rouse up sudden, and say what was that. And all bein now awake did lissen hard, but did hear nought. Then John's mother quissing Sarah, she did say a sort of bump, and nought else, and me thinking she did dream it did say it was but the wind. We bein well awake now do drink some warm cider and eat a piece of plum cake, and fell to talking, and me asking Carter's wiffe if ought else had been stolen in the village, she did say no; but that George Smith should say that he did see a great tall feller by Mary Ann Preces wash house, and later she did find some of her fire logges gone. While we did talk, cums a great bigge crash from the larder and we did start up with fright. Then Carters wiffe did get the big iron poker and saying she would soon settel with the thief, and saying to us to come on, we did catch up some stout stickes and follow her, but verrie cautious. And Carters wiffe bidding us to stand by, did call to the thief to cum out, we knowing he be there. But we hearing no sound did say she should open the door and bid us to hit the thief hard if he did bounce out at us.

SAD NEWS OF FARMER ELLIS

Then she did open the door cannilie, and the thief did in very truth cum out, but we did not hit him for it was nought but John's mother's old tom cat who had got in to steal the good things on the shelves and had smashed some dishes thereby. So we back to the kitchen to have a hearty laffe at our great scare. After telling Carter's wiffe to clean up the mess of brocken crocks. And Sarah boiling the kettel, we did drink a good cup of tea, and it bein now four of the clocke, me and Sarah to the dairy to get the milk pans readie for the morn's milk. And later cums John with the news that Master Ellis be verrie bad, the doctor not sure what to make of him, but did bleed him well for his good.

I be verrie sorrie to hear this, for he were verrie good to help me any time.

Feb. ye 16. – Cums a boy to say Master Ellis be like to die, so John and his mother off there to give what help they can, and later cums a message to say he be passed away; and anon cums John to say his mother be stopping with Mistress Ellis till Mary do cum, he sending Tim with the cart to fetch her.

A JOKE FOR JOHN

Later cums Mistress Prue and her sister, who be verrie sorry when they do hear the news, they saying not to have heard the bell toll. And Mistress Prue off to see what help she can give. Then me and Sarah to divers jobbes. I do miss John's mother a great lot, and shall be verrie glad when she do cum home agen, for she do always seem to make the house the brighter for being in it, bless her.

John in to tea, and do tell him of how we did catch the thief, at which he did laffe right heartilie, but be verrie vexed at the breaking of my dishes.

Then he off to look at Mistress Ellises yards to see all is safe, and me and Sarah to the sewing of sum boddie linen, till John did cum back, then supper and to bed.

MISTRESS ELLIS SELLS HER FARM

᪥

Feb. ye 19. – Master Ellis was buried yesterdaye. It was verrie sad to John and me to see our old friend and naybor put away; but la, we must all cum to the end some time, life be but a little thing, and I do wonder whiles what do lie beyond. But we shall all see anon.

Mary did look very shabby wearing the same black clothes as at her grand dam's burying cum 6 year agon. I did see Emma Trinder and Jane Price in the church yarde, seemingly good friends but without doubt they will be fighting again to-morrow for they be always aquarelling with one another. I did go to look to my dear lady's tomb, which be verrie neat always. I did see the snow droppes were out that I did plant last year, as pure and white as she was her self always.

A COW FOR JOHN

Then we home and I verrie glad it be all over for I like not a burying, and now I have got John's dear Mother back home, and I be verrie glad, for we did miss her sorely this few days. I know not what Mistress Ellis will do now, but John will know anon.

Feb. ye 21. – John in from the yardes to say Mistress Ellis do want him to go to see her, and he off. But cums back later to say she be selling all and going to live with Mary, she not liking the farm. So it is to be sold and John is to have one of her best cowes for his trouble for helping her. I do wonder who we shall have as naybours when she be gone. I like not these changes.

It be verrie pleasant to have John's mother back home, for I do love to look at her sweet old face. I do hope when I do grow as old as she, I shall be as good, bless her.

SARAH IS TO MARRY

Later cums Sarah with a little letter she did have from Passon's mother asking her to drink tea with her, and I do tell her to go, which she do after doing divers jobbes to save me trouble.

Then me and mother to talking, and she do say she be verrie sorry for poor Mistress Ellis, she fearing there be little monies but what the farm do make; and says she, that she will help if they need it, with her own monie; and I did agree it being her own to do as she wills.

Then we to talking of Sarah who be now going to wed Passon cum later, and she did say she must look to her linnen chest and see what will do for her, and thinks she will give her some silver forks and spoons, and a silver dish which I do think be verrie kind. I know not what I shall give her, but later I shall take counsel of John's mother, then I shall do verrie well.

A PARTY FOR CHURCH

Feb. ye 24. – We to church this even, we not going for some while, for Passon do have the services any whiles, and it do be awkward for us to go regularly.

I did see Alice Bachler be home from her place, but not so verrie tidie, and I thought her skin did look very brown for lack of water. Not like my Sarah who be all cream and roses – as John's mother do laffe at her and say.

Everie boddie do know now that she be going to wed Passon, for she did sit with his mother in church, and a fine

118

daintie lass she did look, and verrie different to the village wenches.

THE FARM IS SOLD

Then we home, taking with Mistress Prue, and her sister and Passon and his mother, but I did whisper to him to take Sarah walking, it being fine ānd a moon, and to come in later, knowing well that they do wish to talk by their selves, as I did when John did courte me. So off they did go, and not missed till we indoors. Then I do tell them, and they say quite right and laffe much. But Passon's mother did tell me aside that she did think it verrie kind of me, and she verrie pleased thereby.

Then after all be gone, John do tell me Mistress Ellis be selling her house and land to a farmer up to Cepstowe, but she do not know them at all, they paying her a good price. The name be Jones. I be glad for her, for she will have some what to live on, and not be pennie-less, as we feared. Then John did say should he tell Mistress and Mary to sleep with us the while he and she do settle things and his mother being willing, I be also: and Sarah saying she willing to do anything for their comfort, it be settled for John's mother to go cum morn, and fix it.

Then, all locked up safe, we to bed, it being 9 of the clock.

Feb. ye 28. – We did get our first little lamb this morn; it be verrie ungainly, and be all legs, and verrie sillie. But, la, I do love the little things. The shepherd in later for his 'footing', and John out I do give him his crown piece, as well as a good drink of my primmie rose wine, and a good lump of plum cake; this being the custom in our parts, at the birth of the first lamb, and we do always do so for fear many lambs should die, as may happen if we do not do so.

John have let the shepherd have a bed of clean straw to lie

up on in the corn barn, so we not plagued with him in the house this lambing time, for which I be verrie glad.

Mistress Ellis and Mary be leaving us cum tomorrow, all things being now settled. The new man taking all stock and so on, so there be no sale.

We have got the white cowe which was their best milker as well as a mostly new wagon, and a score of laying hens and a cock which do now fight all the others in the hen house.

A FINE OAK DRESSER

John's mother did also buy privily a fine oak dresser and arm chair, for Sarah cum later, but she not knowing so yet a-while. Mistress Ellis did talk of nought else but her man, and how good he was to her, and did cry much but John's mother do say let her be, for she will be the better for it, and her grief not so hard to bear. She will be well cared for by Mary.

✌ 23 ✌

COUSIN NED VISITS THE HUGHES

✌

The new farmer do cum to Ellises next week, and his man be there already to look to things genst his cumming. I be glad to hear that the shepherd and carter be stopping to work for him, for they would like not to change, being settled there this many years. Passon and his mother and divers others be coming to bid them farewell, so I must now stop and go to the work.

The Passon do make many journeys up here seeminly to see John, but I fear Sarah do see him the longest.

*

March ye 2. – Mistress Ellis and Mary did go yester-morn; John sending them in his little waine with their chests, and riding a piece with them to see them safe on their journey. She did give Sarah a verrie nice set of dishes, and 2 linen clothes for her table, as well as some jugs; and Mary did give her a verrie nice patchie bed cover, with which Sarah was verrie pleased. She be getting quite a store of things for when she do want them. She be liked by everie body in the place and be getting many useful bittes to her furnishing. I do not like to think of her leaving me, but I fear I must get used to it, but I like not to think of her going. She did tell me but yesterday that Passon's mother may later wed her old friend Jasper Carr and go away to live in Gloster town, which be a mighty long way, and that Passon do say he will wed her the same time, but he be cumming to talk to John, and ask what he do think, which be a verrie right and proper thing to do, and me telling John's mother later, she do say quite right also.

JOHN TAKES A TUMBLE

March ye 6. – Today we did have a mightie ado which did cause us much laffter, for John did fall with a mightie bump and sploshing into the muck heap and was verrie wroth thereby. Hearing much noise to the yarde, we out, and there sat John, right to his neck in soft muck, and young Jim laffing fit to buste, the while John did try to get out. Upon which Mother did get a long stick and hold to him, bidden him hold fast the stick while she did pull. So we all to the pullen; he soon out in a sorrie messe, and smellen like a cow pen. Then his mother, after rating young Jim soundlie for laffing at his master, did say to John to go to the back house, not the kitchen, and he did strip off all his clothes, and wash verrie hard to get rid of the stink; the while I did take him more cleen clothes, albeit with a verrie straight face, knowing he be verrie wroth by his mutterings, yet I wanting to laffe hard when I did think of how he did look.

Later when clean and with drie clothes to his back, he to the kitchen where his mother was reddie with a drink of currant wine for his comfort. He did still smell of the stink, but we being wise did keep our counsel. Then me askin how it did cum about, he did say that he did slip through the hole in the tollett floor when letting down a bag of chaffe to young Jim, and so did sit in the muck.

He off again, we did have our laffe out, and then to work at divers jobs; John being verrie wroth all the day, we did tread verrie warily, but, after a good supper he better, and most of the stink gone.

March ye 8. – Cums today a letter from Cousin Ned to say he be cummen to pay us a visit, at which I be verrie pleased; and saying so to John he do say he be too. And later Sarah and John's mother bussie at the cleaning of the house, and me to much cooking, knowing he be a hearty eater.

Carters wife did choppe the heads off two fat cocks, as well as 2 fat geese, and did clean them ready for the stuffen; and I did boil a 20 pound ham as well, and did make a great stock of bred and pies and oddses, the while John did put tap to a keg of new beere.

So now we be ready for Cousin Ned's cummen. I be verrie fond of Cousin Ned, and verrie pleased he can come avisiten us. All bein tired we to bed earlie.

March ye 10. – Cousin Ned did cum earlie this morne, and did do justice to a good breakfast; he eating 4 fried eggs an many slivers of ham, as well as a loaf of my new bred, washen all down with a jug of warm cyder, he bein hungry with so much riding, he cummen a vast way, near 40 miles or more, and not stopped on the way, so he lucky.

Later he out with John and we bussie at divers jobbes, the while Sarah did feed the calves and pigges.

A STEW WITH APPLES

We did have a good hot dinner. John's mother did make a dish she did say was a stew, using up many bittes and oddses thereto, and dumplings and potatoes, all in one pot. I not making any like it, she did show me how.

You do take 4 bigge onions, and cut verrie small, then some potatoes, a measureful, and skin and chop up like wise, then some parsley and sweet bassel and marie golde flowers, that we did dry last year.

This all put in the potte to boil, after putting a good measure of sweet milk. This must boil verrie softly for an hour of the clocke; then put in also, 4 apples chopped small, and any bittes of meat of all sorts, cut in little pieces, and cover with pepper and salt; and put in also the dumplings, made with some flour and chopped fat, mixed verrie stiffe with some milk, then broken in little pieces.

Then it do all boil verrie softly for another 30 minutes of the clock. Then you do mix enough flour and milk together till it be like thick milk, and stir in all and so make it verrie thick.

THEIR SECRET ERRAND

Later cums Mistress Prue to say Emily Lewis be ill and no vittals in the house and that her man be gone God knows where. So me to see what can be spared from the larder, and later off with Mistress Prue to see what's ado. Emily be but a poor shiftless body, and her house be the same, but I did feel verrie sorrie for her, having no bed to lie on, nought but some bagges and her man's old coat for a pillow to her bed. We did give her some vittals to eat, and Mistress Prue did wash her face which was verrie dirty, her hands likewise; and me saying where was her man gone, she did start to cry and say she knows not, but she fears he be gone for good, which be a fine state of things. Then we off after comforting her a bit, and me back home do tell John's mother, who do say poor soul, we must do what we can.

Then John not in, I do tell Cousin Ned, and he saying he will do anything to help, John's mother do say for him to take some firing to warm the poor wretch. So me and Ned off by back ways for John not to see us, and so to the cott with some coals and a warm blanket, and a jug of milk.

Then we back home, me verrie thankful that John be not in to ask our doings, for he likes not to give ought away; and Cousin Ned vowing to keep all quiet, I verrie glad thereby.

❧ 24 ❧

JOHN TAKES UMBRAGE

❧

March ye 13. – I have been verrie bussie this two days, what with the cooking and looking to Emily Lewis, who be much better. I fear she was but nigh clemmed for lack of food. Cousin Ned have bin verrie useful carrying this and that.

John be verrie glum and I know not the why-fore, but he do answer me verrie short and when Cousin Ned did say a word to him, he up and out saying nought, at which Ned do wonder much why. I did ask John's mother what's ado, but she knows nought, and Sarah did say the same, but fears he be not well. Later, when we to our bed chamber I do say what be wrong, but he do bounce into bed and not answer, at which I be verrie pusselled, and know not what to think, or what can be agaite, so me verrie worried.

A SET-TO WITH JOHN

March ye 15. – Such a to do did we have cum yesterday. John being verrie wroth still, I do say to him what be wrong, where on he did cast at me a mighty savage look, and he off without answering, and did bang the door with a mightie bump.

I did ask John's mother, but she did know nought, but says she tackel him and find out first chance. So me getting him later in the kitchen I did say, what was the matter, where-on he did make for the door, but I did get in front, thereby stoping him. Then said I, why is he so churlish with us all, even Cousin Ned, who had been verrie helpful since he cum. Then says he, it be time he be gone from us, cummen atween a man and his wiffe. At this I do nought but stare, not knowing the answer; then says John's mother whatever next will he say, and me being struck by the verrie silliness of it, do nigh burst with laffing. At which he be so wroth he do start to shake me, and me laffing so hard be not able to stop him, till his mother do give him a mighty smack on his ear, and he did let me go.

HIS MOTHER EXPLAINS

Then said she, he should be ashamed to do so to such a faithful wiffe as me, and he not half a man, but just a sotte, always ready for a scratting.

Then she says, out with it, and let us know what it be all about. Then John did say what right had Cousin Ned to taking me walking every day, when I should be at the yardes, feeding the pigges. At which his mother do say what a fool he is when all that had been done was a good turn to one in need. Then said Sarah, fetch Master Ned, and the master can soon see all I had been doing; and she off out, and later Ned cum in and do tell John what we had done to help a poor wretch in need; and said he to John, that if he did but think of others with his heart instead of always his pocket, he would be the better for it. For, said he, he had got a better wiffe than any he did know, and he should be ashamed to speak so. At this John did look verrie sheepish, and did say what could a man think when he did see a man a dandering with his wiffe. At which I so wroth at such talk, did slappe his face sharply, to his great hurt. Whereon his mother says enough of this sillie rubbish, and for John to ask me and Cousin Ned to parden him his folly, and this he did, albeit verrie sulkie.

COUSIN NED OFF AGAIN

But when he gone out, Lord how we did laffe, for what would I be wanting another man for, when already plagued with John, for he be as much as I can manage, and I do still laffe much at his being jealous of Cousin Ned.

March ye 20. – I have been so bussie I could not write in my book before, but John and his mother be out to visit Mistress Webb at Grange Gaites, so while Sarah do sew the while I do write this. Cousin Ned did go cum yesterday, saying he must be back to his shoppe, and he did promise to send Sarah some linnen for her sewing, ready for her bridal cheste. John and he did part verrie good friends, at the last, and he did tell Ned to pay us another visit anon, to which he did say slily; verrie like he would if ever in need of a good wiffe or a bit of dandering. At which John did laffe, albeit not verrie hearty.

Ned did give Sarah a crowne piece for her stocking, which pleased her much, she saying she do like him much. He being always respectful to her.

EWE AND TWO LAMBS

She did find the first violet today, so later we must get some for the drying for puddings. It be verrie cold, and much frost thereby, so we do have a good fire to sit by at nights, and John's mother do put the warming pannes in the beds, which be a great comfort.

Sarah says that Mistress Cross will be wed later on, so I must be ready to let Sarah go before long, but I did beg her to stoppe as long as she can, which she promised. I fear I shall like not for her to go, she be so sensible and verrie clean at work and always to be trusted.

Passon do make many journies here just to talk to John, he do say, but I doubt it.

Later we did get some hotte toddie ready for John and his mother, and they back and warmed, we to bed.

March ye 22. – Today John did grumble much of the colde, and liked not leave the warm kitchen to go to the yardes and me being verrie bussie can write no more today.

We did have a ewe and her two lambs die today, it be a great loss to our pockets.

25

A 'FLIGHTY BIT' AT THE ELLISES

March ye 29. – John have been abed this three days, having a verrie bad chille, and a fine job we be having to keep him in it. If we do leave him a bit, he be out after his smalle cloes, vowing he will go to the yardes, which do worrie him much. But we be doing verrie well, for John's mother do see to all. I know not what we should do without her, she be so good. John mislikes his vittals, the doctor do say to give him milk and gruel, and such messes; and he no meat cum 2 days; at which he do cuss so, and I do always expect to have the bowls of gruel flung at me, and to find the bowl sitting on my head top, for he be like a great fractious baby, and he verrie apt at throwing things in his tantrums. This morn his mother did take away all his cloes, so if he do want to get out, there be nought for him to put on.

'GET ON WITH THE STARVING'

Doctor be cummen in the morn to do sum blood letting, a messie job that I mislike much, but must put up with. John do say he have great pain to his innerds which be all for lack

128

of good feed. But I do not lissen, knowing verrie well it be make believe for all his groaning.

Today he did say I be but starving him, so he can be got rid of out of the way to make room for Cousin Ned, at which I do say to him, get on with the starving, then; and he so astounded at being took up so quick, did only stare at me and said not a word. I have no more time for writing now. I do keep my book in John's mother's chamber, for I know not what he would say if he did know aught of me writing our doings most days. I shall be verrie glad when he down stairs again. We do have much running to and fro to keep eye on him.

April ye 4. – John better and down stairs, but not out doors till cum today, when I did put old Bess to the cart shafts and take him to see the sheep and lambs which be doing verrie well, and no more to come now.

NEWS OF THE NEWCOMER

John did like the outing much, for the sun did shine and was nice and warm. Then we to the yardes, to look at the cows and pigges and feeding bullocks, and John did praise me and his mother much for our keeping all so tidie, for he likes not to see the yards in a muddle.

Then we in to find Sarah ready with the tea on the table, and a nice platter of eggs and ham for John, which pleased him mightilie, for he do love good things to his stummick; and later, after fastening all up safe, we to bed.

April ye 6. – Today did come passon's mother to take tea with us, and to stoppe the night, passon being away to his uncle's till tomorrow, and later did cum Mistress Prue and her sister for companie.

She did say she had seen the new Mistress up at Master Ellises place, and do think her a flightie bit, being verrie dreste up and do try to talk like a fine lady. She do say that she be not at all pretty, but a good figure.

I must look out when I be in church and see what she be like. Then we talking of poor Master Ellis, for we do miss him much, he bein a good neighbour and ever ready to help anybody. Then supper over, John and his mother off with Mistress Prue and her sister, to see them safe home, it bein dark, and me and Mistress Cross to cracken of this and that. She did say that her own wedding will be in two months' time, and why not Sarah and her lad's same time. But, said I, to leave it to them. So we left it. Then they back, we do have a glass of wine and to bed.

April ye 8. – Cums carters wiffe to the washen of cloes, at 4 of the clock, and the day fine it soon out to the drying. Then she to the yardes to clean out the pigges and calves, and in anon to say a calf be sick, and John's mother out to see. She in later do say it be nought but too much milk, and best to starve him a while. And she out to give him a dose of carrie-way and cloves crushed up and put in a lump of butter, which did soon cure the blowing.

Later I did quizz carters wiffe if she have seen the new wiffe up to Farmer Ellises place; and she did say to be sure, but that she did not like her, she bein a uppish madam, and her nose in the air.

A PENNY A DAY

She did say she be verrie dreste up, and do mince along in a way as never was; and that Mary Ann Thomas did tell her that she had been to her to ask her to work dayes, but she did say no, being offered but a pennie a day.

Then John cummen in, we do say no more, and I to

getting him a mug of eldern berrie wine. Then he out and later carters wiffe home with sum oddses for her eating from the larder. And when all work finnished we to the sewing of sheets for Sarah's linnen cheste; then supper and to bed.

John did say he was tired.

April ye 10. – I did get a glimpse of Madam from up to Farmer Ellises place today, when I did go to see sheppards wife who be gone to bed with her tenth child.

THIS VERY PRETTY DISH

I do not like the look of the new neighbour, so I did not speak; not wishing her to think me a villager; I did go to the other side of the street and do carrie my head high. I do not think her verrie well dreste, the colours be verrie bright, but the style was nought. I doubt if we shall ever be friends, so shall not visit her; to be sure we be much better family, so do not mix with all new comers, so I shall not push in nor fuss them. John do not work verrie hard yet, he bein still weak from his blood letting a while agon, so his mother to cook him lots of little messes to give him strength. She did cook a verrie pretty dish today, like this way:

You do take 6 eggs and beat up for five minutes, then chop 4 bigge apples verrie small, and put in a bake pan. Then cover with some good slivers of ham. Cover this with sweet herbs and onion chopt small, some pepper and salt, and cover all with the beaten up egges, then cook in the oven for 18 minutes of the clock, or a bit more if the oven be not too hot.

26

JOHN'S MOTHER OPENS HER PANSY WINE

✌

John's mother did make a rabbit pudding like this and it was verrie tastie. You do take off his jacket and pull out the innerds, then wash verrie clean, and cut up in bittes, and lay them in a pan of warm milk for one hour of the clock. Then mix some pudding flour and butter to a stiff dough and put on the inside of a big basin, keeping a lump to cover all when ready. Then choppe an onion verrie small and lay in the bottom of the basin, then some rabbit, then some fat bacon slices; then more rabbit bittes, which you do cover with some chopt parslie and thyme, and pepper and salt; then more rabbit and bacon till the basin be full.

Then to a measure of hot water put a little measure of beste brandie, and one of vinegar, and pour over all. Then cover all with the dough, tie a clean cloth over verrie tight, and boil for 3 hours and be verrie sure the water be boiling all the time, when it should be cooked verrie well.

This makes good eating with sum boiled cabbage and pertaties, and with a good pudding to follow, do make a good dinner with a jug of cider to wash it downwards.

WITH RIBBON A-DANDERING

April ye 12. – We to church this evening, but I fear we shall not go many more times at week nights, for we shall be bussie at this and that. I did see Sarah Anne Plummer was there, tossing her head about, on which was a new bonnet, that I doubte be paid for: she being a shiftless body. I did also spot Mistress Jones from up at Master Ellises place, verrie high and mighty and aping the great lady, she wearing a verrie queer head covering, like a platter, albeit not so big, with great store of flowers upon it, and ribbon adandering therefrom; in which she did look a sight to be sure. She did also wear a bright red gown of a cottony stuff, and not silk as I could see verrie well, and she did throw off her cloak to show her finery, but la 'twas but trumperie stuff, and not near so good as Sarah do wear.

Shepperds baby was also christened to the name of John Adam, the first to John's honour, shepherd knowing well what a fine man he be for his master.

THREE BEASTS FOR MARKET

Later we back home and to see all safe in the yards, where all the stock be doing verrie well, and John did say he must away to market come next week with three fat beasts, but that he fears much he will not make profit out of them; but that be an old tale we do hear every time he goes to market, so I take no notice thereat.

We indoors later to find Sarah be come in and with supper ready. So John to the cellar for a jug of beer for his own drinking, and his mother and me and Sarah to drink a glass of metheglin which be now good drinking and verrie headie. Then to bed. The days be getting longer now, and so we with more work to do.

April ye 14. – Today being fine me and John's mother to Blackstone Wood to see if the primmie roses be out, and did find it be still early, they being but the little buds, so we just wait a while. So we to the picking of violets for drying, of which there be a great store.

Then we back home ready for the calf feeding, and later John's mother did say, with such great store of violets we need no more. Then John cummen in she do say to wait a minute, the while she go to her bigge cheste, and later she back with a bottle of wine which she did bid him to stopper for her, and did get three of my little glasses and did tell us to sample it. This we did, and we verrie pusselled to know what it be. Then said Sarah, please to tell us what it be, and she did say pansy wine, what she had brought with her when she cum, and forgot till she did see the violets. Me liking the flavour did ask how it be done: and this is the way.

THE MAKING OF PANSY WINE

You do take a peck measure of the fresh picked pansies, the white or purple ones be best, and lay in the warm sun for three days. Then put in a tub and cover all with sugar and ginger powder, and put in one good measure of brandie. Leave to stand for three days, but you must stir hard each day. Then strayne in a muslin cloth and to each pint measure of liquor add 3 lemons cut up, 3 oranges, and 4 big apples; and pour over all a gallon water that has been boiled, and be just warm. Cover over and leave for three more days, then strayne and to each middel [half a gallon] measure add a pint of best brandie and 4 white egge shells which must be verrie clene. Let stand till settled, then strayne once more and put in a keg and fasten down tight when it do no longer bubbel.

INVITATION FROM PARSON

John did beg for more to taste, but his mother did say no, it bein too strong, as indeed was true, for it did make my head to busse, and the chairs to dance, so that I did go to my bed chamber and rest a while, as did Sarah, at which John's mother did laffe right heartilie.

I did also find a daffie dillie in the garden patch today.

*

April ye 19. – Today cum Passon to ask us to his house cum tomorrow night for a partie, he saying his mother's next husband be cum and wishing to meet us, and I did send him to Sarah for sum love making the while I did seek John and his mother to see what they do say to it. They both willen, me back to say so, albeit verrie warie lest they be still at their love making, so did make a clatter to warn them of my cummen. Then telling Sarah to bring Passon a glass of wine and a lump of plum cake, I did quizz who would be at the partie, and he did say Mistress Prue and her sister, and his Aunt Tomsun from Hereford, who be on a visit, and Master Ferris and his mistress, also a Cousin Mattie Strange, as well. After divers talke he off, and we to our work.

❦ 27 ❦

TWO BETROTHALS AT ONE PARTY

❦

April ye 21. – We did go to the partie and did have a merrie time; there being strangers we did put on our beste cloes, and verrie fine we did look to be sure.

John did wear his purpel velvitt small cloes, and sylke weskitt with the gold flowers, and a velvitt top coat, and his best white sylke stock collar all trimmed with lace, his sylke stockens and silver buckeled shoes. He did look verrie grand. John's mother did put on a verrie fine grey sylke gowne with much black lace upon it, and did also wear a black sylke shawl with a fringe of black beads, white sylke stockens and black shoes; also a black straw bonnet with white roses upon it, and she did look verrie sweet, bein such a daintie body.

I did wear my black sylke gown with the white spottes, on which Johns mother did stick some verrie fine lace; and I did wear my dear lady's red necklace of stones, which do shine verrie fine in the light of the tapers, like red fire.

Then Sarah asking me what was best for her to wear, me to my cheste for a gown to becum her. We did hit upon a verrie pretty pinkie sylke with little roses on it, which did suit her verrie well. Then John's mother did pin on it a silver brooch, and gave her some shoes with some buckels on them, and she did look verrie good.

Then leaving carters wiffe to care for the house we off at last, John grumbling that his shoes did pinch like the verrie old nick, but we did take no notice, for he do allus make a fuss and bother over nought.

It bein dry we did walk to Mistress Crosses where we did find Mistress Prue and her sister already, also Master and Mistress Ferris, and all ready with some wine genst our cummen.

THE BRIDES-TO-BE

Mistress Cross did present us to her new man, saying he was Jacob, and I know not his other name, but no doubt shall anon. Then Passon did take me and Sarah to his Aunt and cousin, and I could see Sarah did strike them verrie favourably with her modest ways. Then we to talking of this and that, the men about how things did go, and Master Jacob did say we be verrie lucky to be living in the countrie with the monies sure to our pockets, whiles he do have great work to get paid for his goods. Then said John why not cum here to settel, but no, said he, he liked bussell and seeing plentie; and did laffe right hearty. He be a verrie naybourly sort, with a jolly red face and I did like him much.

Then we to a good supper, the vittals bein verrie good and plentie, and well cooked, so we did all do justice. There was much laffing and cabbel, till Master Jacob did stand up and say: silence the while he did say something to us, at which we do all cool down.

Then said he, fill up the glasses and drink the health of his new bride to be, and this we do with much plesure. Then said Mistress Cross all must drink a health to her son and the best little wench who ever lived, and who she did welcome as a dear daughter. At which there was much laffing at Sarah's red cheeks, and cries of good luck to you both, and she did behave verrie modest. Then said Master Jacob he was verrie proud of his son and daughter that would soon belong to him, and we did all drink to their future.

MASTER JACOB'S RICHES

Then Sarah did stand up and did say thank all verrie much, but she did think all the praise should go to the dear mistress who had done so much for her, bein not only her mistress but her dear respected friend; for, said she, it was a happy home with us, and we one and all good to her, and she did love us all; and indeed, said she, she would not have wed any body and to go away from us, she was so happy with us, and God bless them all three. And I did see tears in her eyes when the silly wench sat down, and there was some in my own as well, for we do like her much, and she do deserve all that be good, as John did stand up to say; for, said he, she had worked well and always done her duty, and we trusted her in all things; and when she was wed later we would miss her verrie bad.

Then we did all drink their health, touching glasses, over and again.

Then Passon out to the kitchen to bring in Joe Smith with his fiddel, and he striking up we to dancing which we did keep up for some time; then we did rest awhile and master Jacob did tell us of his business, which be a paying one, so he have got a warm pocket; and, said he, he was a happy man now for he had gained a son and daughter as well as a wife to leave it all to some day, which I do think be verrie right and proper, but I think should not have been put so plain, Sarah being still my maid and not yet wed to Passon.

Then later, it bein 11 of the clocke, we did put on our cloaks and home. I fear John did find the wine somewhat heady, for he did wobbel much, and did say what's ado with the road, for it did go up and down agen, and he with it. At which we did laffe much, and we soon home where carters wiffe had got a kettle boiling on the hobbe ready for our use if wanted. Then John did say he would have some brandie which he did; then said he where was the stairs, they bein gone, and vowing they was in a new place; at which, after much pushing on our part he be up safe to our bed chamber, and his mother laffing at his silliness did give him a sound smack on his back part and bid him get to sleep, which he did, and we soon settled for the night.

April ye 27. – Today cums the news that Farmer Ferris at Uplands has had trouble with one of his work men, and he bidden him be gone, the man did say let Master Ferris wait a bit and he would let him know. And yesterday night his corn ricks was set afire, and all burned away; and Farmer Ferris do say it be the man Pryce what done it. And he to his cott earlie this morn, did find the man gone and the cott empty.

BLUE HEIFER SLIPS HER CALF

It be verrie bad to lose the corn, and I do wonder much where the man be gone, and do feel verrie sorry for him; knowing Farmer Ferris be a hard man to work for, and no respect for his men, using them like so many tools. John in later to say the blue heifer did slip a dead calf, and he verrie cross thereby, saying he would soon lose his all at this rate; but I answered nought, knowing his ways and Sarah did bring him a messe of eldern berrie wine, saying she was sure he could drink it after being so tired, and he saying she was a good wench did drink it up and off out agen. Then I did laffe at Sarah and say she be nought but a sly baggidge, at which she did laffe also and say a man like the master was all the better for a bitte of fussing, and I did laffe with her, knowing it to be true.

✍🐍 28 ✍🐍

JACK THE PACK-MAN PAYS A VISIT

✍🐍

April ye 29. – Farmer Ferris here this morn to ask if we had seen ought of his 3 milk cowes, he not being able to find them, but we had seen nought of them. Then said he it be that man Pryce, who must be here some place, and we saying we do know nought one way or tother, he off vowing what he would do if he did catch him.

Later John in to say the heifer be full of fever and she must have a draught, and his mother did make one of anniseed and dried clover blows and some ginger put in some warm gruel, which be verrie good for cowes with a fever, and with nought to drink for a day.

Then said John's mother she did hope the man Pryce would get away, for what chance had he against such spite, to which I did agree, for indeed the poor folks do have but little chance against their betters. I be verrie glad I be not one of the poor wretches.

MAY DAY CALLS

May ye 1. – I did have many calls for a May Day cake, the children do always cum, bein sure of an apple as well. Later cum Jack the pack-man with his bag, and he did also carrie for Sarah a bundle from Cousin Ned, he taking the chance to send it this way. Sarah did carrie it to the parlour to see what be in the pack bagges, the while John's mother did fetch the man a jug of cyder and a lump of bread and cheese to eat while we did look to see what he had got. But twas but trumperie stuff, and not good enough for the likes of us; but he had got a verrie pretty blue bead necklace which John's mother did buy for Sarah, she liking it.

But we did buy nought else, not bein in need, so he off, and later Sarah did unpack her bundle from Cousin Ned, and did find some verrie fine linnen for the making of sheets, and damask for the tablecloths for her tables. And, as well a verrie fine piece of white satin with a little blue flower upon it, and some fine lace for trimming.

There was also a little packet sealed up, and when opened, proved to be a verrie nice gold neck chain with a gold cross upon it, and little blue stones, and a packet written for her to wear it on her wedding day to bring her all the good luck he did wish her.

Then Sarah did say how would she ever be able to thank Master Ned for all his kindness to her, and how verrie good it was of him to send so much for her.

I much fear I must be reconciled to her going from us, but I mislike it verrie much, but John's Mother do say, never mind let her be happy as she can, for she be a good maid and all her life before her, being but young. To which I agree, albeit not verrie willing.

FIXING THE DATE

May ye 3. – Cums Passon to see John this morn, and later John do say that Mistress Cross is to wed Master Jacob cum about three weeks, and that Passon do wish to wed Sarah same time; and me talking it over later with John's mother she do say why not. Then said I, how be I to manage without her; and says she; verrie well with carters wiffe everie day to work. So it be settled, and we must help Sarah all we can, but I do mean to ask her privilie to wait awhile and not be in too much of a hurry. I fear I shall be too bussie to write in my book for some whiles if we be to help Sarah with her sewing and oddses.

*

May ye 16. – I have not writ in my little book for some while, being bussie helping Sarah to sew her house linen, which be almost done now. She have got a goodlie store in her linen chest ready for her own house keeping. I do not think I shall have a maid when she be gone, but shall try out with carters wiffe everie day. I mislike the thought of a new maid to be moidered with.

There be no news of the man Pryce, so he be got away safe, I doubt not.

❦ 29 ❦

ANNE AND SARAH GATHER A SWARM OF BEES

❦

May ye 21. – Cums Mistress Prue and her sister to fetch butter, and a score of eggs for their eating; and did stop to drink tea, so we did gossip of this and that. They tellen us that Em Bartlitt and Sarah Anne Price did have a great row, and Em did knock Sarah Anne sillie, and did nigh kill her, and that tother's man did give her a good walloping for doing so, and did say he would pump water all over her if not off soon. They did also say that old miser Amos be sick and do lie upon all his monies, and not let any body do ought for his comfort, but do fly out at all with his cussing. I fear he be a bad old wretch. They do say he did starve his wiffe till she did die.

Later they off home, and me to the feeding of the calves, and later to cooking sum supper for John, then to the sewing of cloes, and to bed anon.

May ye 24. – Cums Carters wiffe with the news that Amos be took at last, and his son be there to see all, and that he be a close sort, and do tell nought to anybody.

She did say none could step nigh the old wretch. He did cuss all and vow not to die to please anybody. And old Betsie Jones did leave him alone, she bein feared of what she should see and afraid the devil would come for him; so she did get out of the house.

It be a bad end of a verrie sinful man, which he certainly was. John cummen in do say a shuppick be gone and from the barn, and he thinks it be stolen, but no doubt it be put elsewhere and will be found later.

His mother and Sarah to tea drinking with Passon's mother, me and John later to my dear Lady's house to see all be going well, as my lord did wish us to. Then to Passon's house where we did drink a glass of wine and then home and to bed, to be up betimes for the washing cum the morn.

May ye 27. – Today cum Sarah to say the bees be swarming, so me out to find them setting in a gooseberry bush, but verrie wild, so Sarah did get a pot and beat hard with a spoon and did bang them till they did be quiet and did hang in one lump, while we did get a skeppe to house them.

Then, taking carters wiffe we to the housing of them; but la, they did go buzzing round her, till she did dance, getting many stings to her legs, whereon she to the kitchen to rub some salt on to stop the stinging.

LIGHTNING STRIKES A RAM

Then putting the skeppe ready, Sarah did brush them in with her hands, having no fear of the bees, and after covering them with sum wet wrappes, to cool them down, we indoors to divers jobs, and to dinner; when we did laffe heartilie at carters wiffe who could not sit down for the stings to her back seat, and she did vow never to go near a bee again.

I fear she did feel verrie sore at the stinging of her body.

May ye 30. – John did take some ewes and lambs to market, so we to the cleaning of the house place, he bein out of the way; and Sarah did lime wash the dairy, making it to smell verrie sweet. Then out to the pig feeding and milking to get all done by the time John was back. Carters wiffe cleaning up the rick yard did find the lost shuppick under some straw. Then me in to find John's mother busy with his supper, with some slivvers of ham and 4 eggs ready, as well as some for us all, it did smell so good.

Then Sarah in to say the Master be cumen up the road, and with some of the ewes, so we be ready for his grumbling later. But he better after filling his belly with the good things got for him, and a mug of his mother's pansie wine.

I did say the shuppick was found, which pleased him; and after seeing all safe for the night we to bed.

June ye 1. – To-day we did have much thunder and lightning which did strike the big elm tree, and kill our big ram, and John verrie vexed thereby. The thunder did keep on all the day at times, and later much rain did fall and run in a torrent down the road, thereby making much mud. The duck pond be verrie full up, and the ducks and gees be verrie content.

Shepherd and carter and young Jim did have the dead sheep to eat, not having fresh meat to their platters for manie months. John did keep the skin to sell come next market day, and did grumble much, saying we should soon be pennyless at this rate, and have nought else but to tramp the roads.

At which we did laffe at him; and later after doing divers

jdos we to bed, it being still verrie hot and thunderie, so that I bid put the bed chamber window ajar when John asleep.

A FOX ON THE PROWL

June ye 2. – It was so hot today I could not make the butter, so must leave till cooler, but I fear it will not be so good and the butter spoilt thereby.

Carters wiffe cum for the washen of cloes and did say that the Joneses up along at Master Ellises place had had some lambs killed, and others much beaten about and they know not how. And John's mother did say that verrie likely it be a fox or two that did it. I do hope ours will keep safe, for to lose a fat lamb be a great loss to our pockets.

We did have more bees to swarm today, but carters wiffe did not help to house them; she saying she did think of her sore back seat whenever she did hear a bee buzz. So Sarah did do it, and later cum tonight did put them on the stand.

The sun do shine bravely most days, and John did say he will set the men to cutten the grass in lower ground cum tomorrow, it being ready. So we shall have much work to do in the yards.

ᘓ 30 ᘓ

A JUDGEMENT ON THE JONESES

ᘓ

June ye 5. – We have got the two bottom grounds of grass cut, and John do think all can be cut down this week. They all hard at it from cum day light till it be dark. The men do drink much cyder, and eat great lumps of bread and cheese, but all do work with a will.

It be verrie hot and today the sky did look verrie mawsey and John do fear there be more thunder to come.

June ye 10. – This be the first chance I have had to write in my book for nigh a week, we bein verrie busy with the hay, which did make in fine fettel, and we able to stack it verrie quick.

AMOS'S UNKIND COTT

Carters wiffe did say that Farmer Jones did stack much of his hay cum last Sabbeth day, which I do think verrie wrong, and no good ever did cum of such wickedness. She did also tell us that the family what did go to live in old Amoses cott be gone, they saying it be an unkind place, and they getting no rest from the knocking and groans about the place. Which be verrie true for he was a verrie bad old man, and so do not rest for his sins.

Carters wiffe did say also that Josh Privvitt did say he did see old Amos tother night with a lit taper, go down the garden path, and the sight did make him all amuch of sweat and he did make for home as fast as he could, which me knowing him well do not doubt.

June ye 14. – John in for a tot of beer do say Farmer Joneses hayricks did set fire yester night some time and be all burned away, the weather bein verrie fine.

John's mother did say that her rhematiz did pain her much today, and Sarah did make a bread and lemon thyme poultice and put thereto, which did do much good.

John did fuss much, fearing his mother should lie abed, at which she did laffe and say it was nought and soon gone again. Carters wiffe do tell us the Joneses be verrie funny folks, for they do never let a body in to the house place, nor do give their work men ought in wages, but do scrape everie penny for their own pockets.

I doubt if they be much good.

A THEFT DISCOVERED

June ye 16. – John's mother out to the back place this morn did see that a big ham be gone, and a piece from a flitch as well. At which we much pusseled, knowing that the cat could not take so much, so me to the yardes to fetch John to have a look, and he as amazed as we, and not able to say where it be, nor we; so we back to work, it being no use to do ought else. Later carters wiffe in, I do show her, and she did say where is it; which I do think was verrie sillie, me not able to say. So I did tell her to be off and scrub the dairy floor, but I do wonder much where the ham and piece of flitch be gone.

June ye 18. – Cums Passon to see me and John about his wedding Sarah, so we to the parlour to talk, and he do say his mother be all ready to wed, so he do want to fix his own, and why not soon; at which I do say no, and for Sarah to say, and also to give us time to get ready. And John's mother did fetch Sarah to see what she did say, and she knowing my wish about it, did say let me fix it, and she abide by it, which I do think be verrie dutiful of her, and so it do rest for now.

June ye 20. – Cums carters wiffe with the news that the Jones be going to be sold up by a body at Chepstow for monies that he did lend them, and they not paying back, so the people be selling all to get it again.

She do also say that the shepperd there do say he have had but one settel since they did cum, and he and his childer be hungrie through it all, and so I do think it verrie likely it be

he who did fetch the ham and piece of flitch, and so do make
up my mind to find out.

SOME DETECTIVE WORK

Later I do talk to John's mother, and so she and me to the
shepperd's cott, outwardly with a basket of bits for the
children, but also to find out if they did take the ham. They
do make us welcome, saying they be mighty glad of the bits,
for all be hungry and indeed they did look it. Then John's
mother did out with it about the ham verrie sudden, and me
watching hard at them, did see they were verrie struck, but
not guilty; and soon we off, me saying to send them more bits
anon, which I shall do, bein verrie sorry they should go
hungry.

But I still do not know where the ham be got to.

❧ 31 ❧

ANNE MAKES READY FOR A JOURNEY

❧

June ye 23. – John in with the milk this morn did say to us
that Master Evans from the Crown had been up to see him at
the cow yarde, and did say had we lost ought lately. And John
saying why did he ask, Master Evans did say that last night
as ever was, two men did let it out at the Crown to the others,
and if John do like to go at night he verrie likely will hear it
also.

So later when the work all done for the day, John did go to
the Crown by back ways, and landlord did set him down by a
pot hole in the kitchen wall and well hid from all, and nought

knowing. And later he did hear much laffing, and did hear the two men tell the tale of how they did get our big ham and piece of flitch, the while we be abed; and, said they, that they would have more, we having plentie.

THE THIEVES ARE PUNISHED

Then John taking a peep did see that it were Bill Jones from the cross roads and Bert Price from New Lands. So John to the landlord, and begging the use of a good strong whip did tell him to fetch out Bill Jones to the back yarde, and stand by, the while he did pay Jones out for his thievery. And the landlord did bring him, and John catching him by the neck collar did lamme it into him with the whip as hard as he could, and ask him if he would touch ought again. And he saying no never, John did whip him hard till he be off out the gate and for home. Then, when John had got his wind back, landlord did bring out Price, and John did whip him till he did cry for mercy, vowing never to touch ought of his again. Then he off too, verrie glad to get away.

Then John home to tell us all, and me knowing John's way with a whip I doubt the men will have cause to think for many days to cum; and so now we do know where the ham did go.

A WEDDING DATE

June ye 25. – Mistress Cross did cum to-day to say that she be to wed Master Jacob cum the middle of next week; and she did want to take Sarah, and John's mother and me with her as well. At which I did say the others could go, but I must stop home, for what would John do: and privilie me not wanting to go, after she did say she be going to her sister's to be wed, which be a long way from us.

But John coming in, she do say why can I not go, and John

did say, to be sure she can go, albeit I did look at him hard and shake my head for him to see I want not to go. So to please him I did say yes, but I do see no pleasure in it as yet.

AN EARLY START

Sarah do dance about at the thought, she never going away from this place in her life. We shall be gone three whole days, and I fear there will be many muddles to clean up when we come back agen; if we ever do, which I doubt, but they all so set upon it I do give in.

June ye 28. – There have been much bussell and hard work to do, ready for our journey with Mistress Cross, and we do start cum the morn at 4 of the clock, so as to reach the end of our journey before dark, we having to ride nigh 20 miles by road. I shall ride Nancie, and John's mother will ride her own nag Browne Socks, and Sarah will ride in the little waine with Mistress Cross and her baggage she be taking with her, and Passon will ride with us also.

John's mother did say to me to hide my monies carefully for fear we be stopped, so I have put most all in a bag of chaffe, nigh 10 guineas, in the little waine marked with a red string to know which one.

I be verrie tired with so much cooking and cleaning of the house from top to bottom. Mistress Prue and her sister will cum and care for John, and carter's wiffe to do the work. I shall not rite in my little book till I be back which I fear may be never, when I do think of the miles I be going to travel. I do hope if we do meet a robber he will not search in the chaffe bag for my 10 guineas that I did covver up in a cloth, lest they do chink; for I like not to lose monie.

This be the first time I have gone from John's side since we did wed.

John being gone to bring back Mistress Cross and Passon to sleep here to-night, to be reddie cum the morn, I do write in my book the while. John's mother do pack a basket of vittals for our journey, for we shall be riding most of the day, and she do say it be safer to take it with us, than to show our monies where others can see it.

Sarah be in fine fettle, she liking the thought of it all, never going anywhere but to the market in her life.

John's mother cummen in do say they be cummen up the road. I rite no more for we must to bed earlie to be readdie cum the morn. Carter's wife will sleep on the settel to-night to be ready with the breakfast for us so not to hinder the time. I be feered of the journie, but it be best to say nought, but I do wonder if I shall ever rite in my little book agen.

✌ 32 ✌

SARAH TRIES ON HER WEDDING VEIL

✌

July ye 4. – We be back safe and well for which I do thank God. The house place was verrie clean and tidie, Mistress Prue and carter's wiffe doing verrie well; but la, it is good to be home in my own house.

We did hav fine weather and no thunder, for which I was glad, and now I can rite all in my little book, for John be gone to look at a colt he do think of buying from Farmer Ferris, and he do allus stop verrie long to his gossup and cyder drinking, and I have tried much to rite.

We did set out at 4 of the clock after a good breakfast carter's wiffe and Mistress Prue did cook. It was very pleasant out, it being earlie and the sun just cummen out; and we did go alcng at a good pace and did meet divers folks. None did bother us, and so we did reach Mistress Crosses sister's place before dark, and right glad I was to get of Nancie's back and stretch my legs after so much riding.

MUCH FUN AND DANCING

We did rise earlie next day to be readie for the wedding at 11 of the clock. Sarah was a bridesmaid and verrie nice she did look and the prettiest wench of the whole bunch. Passon was verrie proud of her, and all did praise his good taste for a wife; and Master Jacob did say that if it had not been his wedden day to Passon's mother, be danged if he wouldn't marry Sarah.

At which we did all laffe heartilie.

After Passon's mother and Master Jacob were wed there was much eating and drinking and cabbeling, and a right merrie time we did have with much dancing and jigging about, till 12 of the clock middel nite, then we to bed.

Me and Sarah and John's mother did share our bed chamber with divers others, and we did leave a room alone for the bride and her man to share privilie, as was but seemlie.

The sillie wenches was verrie noisie and so we did not get scarce any sleep, but we did laffe much at their antics. One of them did go over with a great bump when she did try to stand upon her head upside downwards.

NEWS OF THE JONESES

Then we up agen verrie earlie in the morn to breakfast, and so readie to start on our journie homewards; me verrie glad to be going back.

I did have a great fright on the way, for a man did step from the road side and stop us, whereon John's mother did point a pistol at him and he did say he wanted nought but to know the way; and passon saying where to, he did tell him, and passon did tell him the way he wanted to go; and he off agen; me so frightened lest he did cum for us, I did watch him till he out of our ken, for I did fear much for my 10 guineas which was still in the chaffe bag.

John was verrie glad to see us home safe and did kiss me and his mother soundlie, and later we to our work.

There was much news for us to hear; Mistress Prue telling us the Joneses house be burned down and all lost, and the man be cum from Chepstow yesterday and did drive away all the stock, and all the implements be took away also. So much do happen in a bit that it do fair amaze us all.

I did give carter's wife a great basket of oddses what Mistress Cross did send for her and she verrie pleased thereby, and we did bring back a lump of cake for Mistress Prue, and her sister. So now I must stop writing, for Sarah do say the master be cummen in. We shall not see Mistress Cross for sum while, she going away with her man to her new house a long way from us.

FAGGERS FROM THE VILLAGE

July ye 6. – John do say the wheat be getting ripe with so much fine weather, so we shall soon be at harvest once agen. He do say there be plenty in the village he can get for the faggen, so we shall not be bothered with the Irish folks this year, and I be verrie glad, for the women was such great trollops and verrie drabbie hussies, what the men did bring. So we must be bussie soon with the baking of bredd as soon as the men do start the cutten.

Carter's wife says she did hear Farmer Ferris be going to

have the land that was Farmer Ellises farm, which be true, John telling Squire we do not want more, we having quite enough.

It do seem that Squire have got the sellen of it. I be now getten readie to let Sarah go, for passon do say he be readie, so he be sleeping here the while carter's wife and Sarah's sister Pam do make his house all sweet and clean for her going.

SARAH GATHERS FURNITURE

We do much sewing when the work be done for the day, but Sarah have got all readie and plentie to her linnen chest, and also a good stock of boddie linen which John's mother did make look verrie fine with lace she did make herself.

It do look verrie good and she did tell Sarah to care always for the underpart and keep it neet and the top would sure to keep so. And Sarah did promise allus to keep it so. Cum tomorrow we going to the passonage to see how it do look now it be cleaned and readie.

July ye 8. – Today John's mother did tell Sarah that the oak table and chair she bought from Mistress Ellis was for her, at which she verrie pleased and did thank her verrie prettie, and give her a great hug and say she be the dearest woman in the world; and so she be, for she be ever doing what she can for others happiness, bless her, and we do all love her for it. Then everything bein put readie Young Tim did take all to the passonage, we going as well to see all be put safe.

The house do look mightie fine now, and when all be in its proper place it will be verrie cumfortable and Sarah sure of a good home.

The wedden be in 3 days from now and we shall be mighty bussie with much cooking. John did say this morn he will kill a fat lamb cum to-morrow and we can have a sucken pig to roast, of which I do hope he will not eat too much, he bein verrie partial to it.

Mistress Prue did bring Sarah's wedden gown which she have made from Cousin Ned's Satin, and it do look verrie nice, all trimmed with the fine lace, and some at the sleeves and throat. She did also bring with her a piece of verrie fine net lace that she did call a wedden veil, and that she do say all ladies of high degree do wear, and she did put it on Sarah and it did look mightie grand. I did like it much. Then putten all away in the chest, we to our work.

❧ 33 ❧

GREAT PREPARATIONS FOR SARAH'S WEDDING

❧

July ye 10. – Yesterday we did do much cooking readie for the wedding cum to-morrow. Carter's wife did wash and press my fine damask table cloths and little napkins, all readie for the tables, and John's mother did make a mighty fine cake putten in many good things to its richness. John did kill the lamb and little pig, and Carter's wife did chop off the heads of 6 fat cocks and also sum ducks.

Squire did also cum this morn to see Sarah and did give her a guinea and me 2 hares, and did drink a glass of wine to her future happiness.

Passon's 2 cousins did cum to-day, also his uncle Tom, to wed them. Mattie and Floe will be maids for Sarah.

And now, there bein much cooking to do, I must go to work and rite more later.

MANY GOOD THINGS

July ye 10 (later). – All the cooking be done and do make a mightie brave show, and now I can rite in my little book agen, where I did have to leave off this morn. Cousin Ned be cum and so we have got a house full, but that be all to the good for there be plentie for all.

John's mother did stuff the little pig and did make it so: take the crumbs from 2 stale loafes of bredd, sum lemon thyme, and parslie chopt verrie fine, 6 big apples also, and 6 eggs boiled verrie hard; then some slivvers of fat bacon that be cooked readie.

This be all mixed up together. Then take 12 fresh eggs and hit up all frothie in a bowl, mix all together and put inside the pig's belly, and fasten up well, so none do fall out in the cooking. Then it be put in the oven and baked for 2 hours.

COUSIN MATTIE'S DISH

We did cook the hares a new way Cousin Mattie did show us and which she says be verrie nice.

She did take off their jackets and take away the guts, then wipe verrie clean, but not wash them. Then did cut them in nice joints, and then she did put a layer in a big stew pot of chopt onions and sweet herbes, such as thyme, parslie and sweet basil and marjorum. Then sum joints of the hares, and more herbes and pepper and salt, then a layer of ham cut in bits, and when half full she did put in 2 sticks of cinnamon. She said we to be verrie sure to do this always, as it do make a fine flavour; then more joints and ham and herbes, till full up. Then she did turn all out in a big pan and strain off the liquor in a littel pan. Then she did take away all the bones and cinnamon sticks and chop up verrie fine and put all in a deep pot and pour over a little measure of the liquor, and press well; then set it aside to get cold on the larder shelf.

The rest of the liquor she did boil in a pan till it be half gone, then she did strain it into a dish to get cold. When reddie she did turn out the hare meat on a dish and cuvver with the jellie chopt up in little bits, and it do look a mightie fine dish all readie for the eating cum to-morrow.

NEW LITTLE CAKES

Cousin Floe not to be outdone have made sum little cakes that was a new way to me. She did get a bowl and put in a measure of flour. Then in another one she did put a pound of my fresh butter and a measure of sugar and beat it all soft and like cream. Then she did drop in, one at a time, 6 eggs and beat all together till mixed up verrie well. Then she did throw in the flour, still beating the mess till all be mixed. Then she did take 2 of my shallow tins and pour the mess in equal lots and bake in the oven for 30 minutes of the clock. Before she did bake them she did chop up sum filber nuts and sow all over the top of both cakes. When these was cooked and got cold she did get sum butter and sugar and raspberrie jam and did beat till soft and did spread it on one of the cakes, then did press tother on top so the mess was between the two, then she did cut in divers shapes and put them on one of John's mother's silver dishes, and mightie good they do look.

LAMB, COCKS AND DUCKS

We did roast the lamb in 4 pieces and the cocks and ducks, and bake manie apple pies and jam tarts and cakes, and I did

157

bring out my silver pepper pots to use as well as my silver salt cellars, and the best forks and glasses be all readie. I be verrie tired having had much to do all day, so I must to bed now where John be asleep this long while.

⋙ 34 ⋙

THE WEDDING, AND ANNE SAYS
GOOD-BYE TO HER BOOK

⋙

July ye 15. – Sarah was wed cum 4 days agon, and a right merrie time we did have. We, all up betimes, did work with a will to get all readie. Mistress Prue did get the tables all set in good time, John's mother helping, and all did look verrie well, there being great store of good things.

Then later we to help Sarah to put on her wedden cloes, it bein all new from shift to gown, and she did look verrie prettie in her satin gown and wearing the gold necklace Cousin Ned did give her. Then Mistress Prue did fasten the wedden veil to her hair and she did look verrie daintie, like a real lady when readie to go to the church.

We did make a goodlie show as we did walk down to the church, where Passon was waiting for us. John did father Sarah and did look verrie smart in his best velvet cloes. His mother did wear her grey silk, while I did put on my blue silk with the yellow lace.

Every boddie did cum to the church to see the wedden, and it over we back home, all going off well at the church. Then the feasting did begin, and all did praise Mattie's way of doing the hares, and also Floe's little cakes.

158

There was much drinking of healths and speechifying. Then did cum a nice surprise for Sarah, for Carter's wife did cum to the parlour to say John was wanted, and he out, did cum back later to say it was a present cum for Sarah and she to go and see it. So we all out with her to see whats agaite, and did see a man with a verrie prettie black ponie, which he did say was for Sarah from Mistress Ellis and Mary, and did give her a letter also, in which they did say the ponie was for her to ride with her new husband and that they did wish her much happiness and a long life.

So she can now company passon when he do ride abroad.

Then after the man did stable the ponie and feed it, he to the kitchen for a platter of good things and a drink of wine before going home agen, and Sarah did rite a letter to thank them, the while I did pack up a basket of good things for him to take to Mistress Ellis and Mary. Then he off, we back in to enjoy ourselfs.

All did eat and drink heartilie, and John did tell all to drink the health of the bride and groom and all did so with much laffing and much passing of bottles and jugs and all did have their fill.

THE VILLAGE REJOICES

Later cum all the village folks to the house shouting and singing and saying good luck to them both, and John did fetch in Shepperd and carter to take out sum jugs of cyder, and carter's wiffe and Jane did cut up much bredd and chees so all could have sum. And later John did bid all to be gone, and we to dancing and much talking, there bein 30 in all at the feast. Before all was over John's mother did make a great bowl of punch and brought in, saying all must drink to the good luck of the young folks just beginning life together.

So each of the visitors did take a drink from the bowl, and Cousin Ned did say that as he couldn't wed Sarah he would wait for her daughter, at which she did blush verrie rosie; but passon did laffe and say 'verrie well it was a bargain then.' Then Sarah did say how much she did owe us, where she had bin verrie happie, and all her life would honour us for it. She did say how much she did want still to be with us, but she did say slyly what could she do with passon so pressing. At which all did clap hands and agree.

It being late by this time everrie boddie did start home, albeit sum a bit jerkie from so much wine drinking, and Master Ferris did say he was going to ride his horse backwards home for the tail was more to hold on to and so steadie him.

SARAH AND PARSON LEAVE

John did kiss all the ladies in spite of the scratting and smacking. Then they all gon, John and Passon to the parlour, the while me and John's mother did go with Sarah to my bed chamber and I did give her the 10 guineas I did not spend at Mistress Crosses wedden for her stocken, knowing she will use it well, as did John's mother.

So she do start her new life with summat to her pocket. Then she did hug us both saying how she should miss us, and that she should allus cum to us for good advise when she did need it, for she did owe us all she had got this day and she loved us all. Then she did hug us agen and later we down stairs and they off to their own home, where I do hope God will bless them both as much as he have me, with a good husband albeit a baby at times; a good home, and above all, a dear mother I can love and honour allus.

I feel I shall miss Sarah but must put up with it. We did have much work to do after all gone, for I could not go to bedd till the dishes were washed and the house place tidie readie for next day. Then bidden Carter's wife and Jane to sleep in Sarah's bed readie for work cum morn we to bed and verrie wearie with so much bussel.

July ye 18. – Today John's mother and me did visit Sarah, and young Jim did also take a flitch of bacon in the little waine, and a couple of pigs for the passon's stye, as well as sum clean straw to bed them. All was verrie tidie and neat and I can see she will be a good wife to passon.

After drinking tea we back home, Sarah walking a piece with us. Then we to the calfe and pig feeding and later to work indoors. I fear I shall not rite much more in my little book for there be more work to be done now the corn harvest be cummen on. Carter's wife do do much work but it be not like having Sarah with us.

WHEAT CUTTING TO-MORROW

July ye 24. – John is going to cut the wheat cum to-morrow so we have made much bredd readie. I have no time to rite in my book now, though I do love it so much, it be like a friend to me. I shall allus be glad that my own dear mother did let Mistress Prue show me how to rite and figure. I have no more time to rite now, I must go to the pig feeding.

August ye 6. – I have not writ in my little book for manie days, not feeling verrie well. John's mother did bid me to cum to my bed chamber to rest, so I do get my book out of the linen chest where it be hid, and do rite. John's mother do think we ought to have another maid, so much hard work bein too much for us and with the child cummen there will be more to do, so I shall not write agen in this book, but I shall keep it for all ways. When I do think back I do know how verrie luckie I be and with so much to be thankful for, and I do hope my children that may cum will sum day see my little book and grow to be as good as their father is.

ANNE SAYS GOOD-BYE

All times I do wonder who will read my book and what will become of it, but I do hope that annie who do read it may be as happie a wife as I be.

So now I say goodbye to my book, for I shall have too much work to do to write agen.